Books by Tom Spears

Non-Fiction
Navigating Corporate Politics
Bad Employee, Great Employee (Coming in 2017)

Fiction

The Carson Series
Leverage
Pursuing Other Opportunities
Outsourced (coming in 2016)

The Smith Series
Deliverables
Heir Apparent
Change Agent (coming in 2018)

The Martin Series
Incentivize
Supply Chain (coming in 2016)

The Priest Series
Synergy
Anergy (coming in 2018)

Other/Stand Alone Novels
Empowered
Right Sized (coming in 2017)

Bad Boss, Great Boss

By Tom Spears

www.tomspears.com

DEDICATION

This book is dedicated to Marion A. "Bud" Keyes IV. Bud was the best boss I ever worked for, and his habits, behaviors, and abilities are the primary source of information for all of the "great boss" examples in this work. Alas, Bud left us on May 17, 2013, and the world is diminished as a result.

ACKNOWLEDGMENTS

This book was originally "written" as a series of blog posts which began in 2011 and were subsequently refined and expanded. Eventually, a fairly complete treatment of the subject was achieved, and plenty of examples were subsequently added to illustrate the points I'm attempting to make.

As I've disguised the identities of the many bosses I've had over the years to protect them from possible errors in my memory, I will not list them here. It would be a grave injustice, however, to not thank them for the experiences they offered me – both positive and negative. While I've abstracted in this work, characterizing bosses as either "good" or "bad," true reality is much more complicated. In my experience, no boss is ever wholly good or completely bad. While each boss had his (yes, they were all men) share of challenging behaviors, most also had a measure of skill and talent, as well.

Gentlemen – thank you for your instruction, both intentional and inadvertent.

As has been true with my other books, I owe a debt of gratitude to high school chum Mike Miller for his incredible proofreading and editing skills. Any errors remaining in the text are undoubtedly mistakes I made after Mike worked on it.

Finally, I thank my immediate family for their support during the writing process.

TABLE OF CONTENTS

Introduction

What this Book Is, and What It Is Not

If you're reading this book in the hopes of learning how to propel yourself up the corporate ladder, you should probably put it down now. This is not a manual describing how you might politic and maneuver in the ruthless and sharp-elbowed space of middle and upper management. Nor will it instruct you in the ways of endearing yourself to those occupying management seats above yours. Both sets of skills are necessary for a successful climb through the management ranks, but they are not the subject of this work.

In fact, this book provides little to no advice on advancing your career, taking on peers and winning, or sucking up to senior management. For insight into these items, you can see my previously published book, *Navigating Corporate Politics*.

If you are perusing these words with the hopes of becoming the best possible supervisor you can be – particularly in the eyes of your subordinates – then you're in the right place. Succinctly put, my objective is to help you become the best possible business leader, a skill that in some ways is at times at cross purposes with career success.

A bit about your author…

So why listen to me? I'm not Jack Welch. I haven't made more money than Warren Buffett, and I don't write with the talent of Stephen King.

While I have never been the CEO of a massive public corporation, I have had the privilege of working for some amazingly skilled and horribly flawed bosses. I've had bosses that literally refused to provide any direct feedback. I've had bosses that tossed subordinate after subordinate under the bus to protect themselves. And I've had bosses that inspired me and earned my undying loyalty. Those experiences and my own educational and vocational background provide a perspective that I believe can be extremely helpful to new managers and seasoned veterans alike.

Over the last 35 years, I have been a serious student of the art and science of management. During that time, I matured from an ambitious young pup with excessive drive and almost no filter to a seasoned General Manager, who was generally liked and respected by my subordinates.

My career began with a decade working in the trenches at a components division of General Motors where I progressed through a series of engineering and low-level supervisory positions. During those years, I had the opportunity to manage peers indirectly (an experience everyone should have at some time in their career), progressed through a series of bosses both good and bad (on of my best and one of my worst both came during this time at GM), and supervised an unruly group of unionized shop-floor employees.

I also had the opportunity to study at the "West Point of Capitalism" (Harvard Business School) while on a GM Fellowship. This experience made me much more aware of the strengths and pitfalls that we, as individuals with our own personal perspectives and experiences, bring to the management task.

A subsequent half-decade was spent at Emerson Electric, arguably one of the greatest manufacturing conglomerates in the world. There I progressed from Analyst to Manager to Vice President, ultimately ending my time at the company as the President of a smallish (200-person) division. During that time, I worked for my greatest boss – you'll find much of the wisdom he imparted to me during those years reflected in these pages.

Emerson taught me many things, including the fact that my personality was incompatible with the company's prevailing culture – one of provocation, constant challenge, and strict "management by the numbers." It was a time when my skills grew substantially – along with my sense of discomfort.

Next, I joined Valmont Industries, a manufacturing company located in Nebraska. While at Valmont, my career progressed from Division President to Group President. Shortly before my decade plus with Valmont came to an abrupt end (my termination as the company carved a path through the first year of the "Great Recession"), I spent a short time as the heir apparent to the CEO.

It was at Valmont where much of what I learned at Emerson and GM was put into practice. Even though I'd had great teachers earlier in my career, there was still a fair amount of trial and error needed before I really understood how to manage. I suspect taking similar risks and making similar errors is something that students of this book will still likely find unavoidable. As the old saying goes: "Some things just have to be learned firsthand." Stick with it long enough, and you will realize that management is an experiential as well as an intellectual endeavor, and there is only so much that can be learned without direct immersion in the process.

While at Valmont, I was blessed with strong teams of subordinates that achieved great results for the company. And although I can't claim that they always got along with one another, I was generally considered by them to be the kind of boss I will describe as "good" in the forthcoming pages.

My final public company experience came as a Division President for Lindsay Corporation, another Nebraska manufacturer. While my stay there was short (less than a year), I was able to add a few more "Bad Boss, Great Boss" experiences to my portfolio.

Following Lindsay, I simultaneously began a career as a writer (hey, if you enjoy fiction and are reading this book, check out my corporate thriller novels at www.tomspears.com) and as an entrepreneur.

As of this writing, I have nine published books and share ownership in two small companies where I operate more like a board member than a day-to-day manager. Even with a career's worth of managerial experience under my belt, I still find myself picking up the occasional pointer – both good and bad. I can't envision the day where I will end my education on the subjects of business and management.

What the book is not

"Bad Boss, Great Boss" is not an exhaustive treatment of the subject of properly managing subordinates. It isn't a treatise on leadership, although leadership (or lack thereof) is certainly an important underlying element of many of the characteristics and behaviors I describe.

This book is also not a rigorously researched academic work. It is, by its nature, anecdotal. There are no studies to back up my conclusions. As you proceed through my observations and recommendations, bear in mind that another person might draw different inferences from the same experiences. You are, by definition, getting my take on things.

What the book aspires to be

Over my career, I've worked for numerous bosses, been a boss myself, and have been an earnest student of leadership. I've also had the opportunity to assess and critique many other bosses as a third-party observer, the result of being involved in more than two dozen acquisitions throughout my career.

This work has been stimulated by the observation that some of the bosses I've known are hated and despised by their subordinates while others (alas, a minority) are loved and revered. Parenthetically, I must also note that success or failure with subordinates appears to be only loosely tied to career success for the manager.

In this context, I've often found myself asking what behaviors did the "Bad Bosses" exhibit that induced such strong negative reactions? What characteristics did the "good bosses" have that drew subordinates in and bound them tightly to their leader? After a career's worth of observation, certain patterns emerged, ones that might not be obvious to a person with less of a penchant for managerial critique or to a person with less experience.

This book is the summation of those observations and conclusions.

How the material is organized

The book is broken into two parts reflecting the two extremes of supervisory capability – Bad Bosses and great bosses. Each part is introduced by a short chapter summarizing a variety of characteristics that can drive the perceptions of a boss to be identified as either "bad" or "great." Subsequent chapters go into greater detail about each of these characteristics and provide examples of how I encountered them in the real world.

The "Bad Boss" portion of the book focuses specifically on a set of behaviors that are present in many bosses to a limited degree, but which, when taken to the extreme, are toxic. Bad-Boss types are characterized by such extreme behavior, and the underlying causes and drivers of that behavior are explored. While you are not likely to see such stark examples in real life (people are much more complicated than these simple abstractions), once you are aware of an extreme management type, you should be better able to spot the attendant behaviors in flesh-and-blood managers.

An interesting point about "Bad-Boss" behaviors – it only takes one of these extreme management characteristics to slot an otherwise "Good Boss" firmly in the "Bad" category. If you aspire to be a "Good Boss" or even a "Great Boss," you'll have to take care to avoid all of these extreme behaviors.

In contrast to the large variety of failure modes explored in the "Bad Boss" portion of the book, the "Great Boss" section focuses on the leadership characteristics of essentially one person (with a few minor contributions from several other bosses I've encountered throughout my career). That one person, M.A. "Bud" Keyes IV, a recently deceased senior manager at Emerson Electric, was the best boss I encountered in my career by a wide margin.

Keyes represented the pinnacle of managerial skill (at least in my opinion), and it was under his tutelage that my own skills as a manager grew and matured. In addition to his senior role at Emerson, Keyes' work history included time spent as CEO of Bailey Controls and as a group executive at McDermott International.

Unlike "Bad Boss," which presents a collection of singular, extreme characteristics that must be avoided at all costs, "Great Boss" enumerates a variety of behaviors any one of which, if consistently exhibited by a manager, will improve his or her leadership performance in the eyes of subordinates.

A "Great Boss" would, of necessity, need to possess many if not all of these abilities.

A word about gender references

I mentioned earlier that all of my bosses have been men. In a world, however, where women increasingly fill managerial roles up and down the organizational ladder, it seemed foolish to me to refer to every boss in every discussion as "he." As a result, I've intermixed "he" and "she" references in the text by using them indiscriminately in alternating chapters. Other than representing an attempt to show gender balance, this has NOT been done in an attempt to identify any particular characteristic as male or female. I did, however, maintain the male gender pronouns throughout the second half of the book, when referring to my Great Boss.

Furthermore, I acknowledge that to the degree men and women manage differently in a broader sense, I could be missing some characteristics (both good and bad) that would be much more frequently reflected in female managers. If such characteristics exist, that is. My best guess, and, mind you, it is only a guess, is that the variations of technique, skill, style, and effectiveness (or lack thereof) within managers in either sex, is substantially broader than any specific differences between them.

You, as the reader, can make your own call on such matters.

How to use this book

I've envisioned "Bad Boss, Great Boss" as a tool managers can use both to recognize and correct pitfalls and to explore and acquire new skills that enhance their leadership abilities. While I would recommend a cover-to-cover reading, any individual topic could easily be explored by locating the desired area of focus in the chapter headings and reading that subject by itself.

The book should also prove to be useful for an employee in the process of searching for a new job. "Boss shopping" is a prudent practice for any prospective employee exploring new opportunities. As the old saying goes, "employees join companies but leave bosses" is, in my experience, largely correct. "Bad Boss, Great Boss" provides plenty of characteristics to search for, and a similar list of others to avoid.

One bit of additional advice to the prospective job searcher – get independent input on your prospective new boss! The entire interview process puts both interviewer and interviewee on their "best behavior" – meaning that plenty of faking is present on both sides of the table. Many times the boss a prospective employee thought she was getting is a far cry from the dysfunctional lunatic to whom she actually end up reporting. Managers are often quite good a hiding their flaws and showing potential hires exactly what they want to see – at least for a short time. Later the truth comes out, but by then it is usually too late.

Check current employees, former employees, peers, or anyone else that has had a chance to see your prospective boss in action. Use "Bad Boss, Great Boss" as a guide to determining which extreme type of leader your future boss might be, then explore how far along the "Great Boss" path he or she has likely progressed. By aggressively boss-shopping, you can avoid one of the pitfalls most likely to cause a future job change.

And maybe in the process, you'll end up with the opportunity to work for a truly Great Boss, a treat to be sure.

Part 1

Bad Boss

Chapter 1

Extreme Leadership Types

While researching one of my novels ("Heir Apparent," for those who might be interested), I found myself exploring several hard-to-work-for leadership styles – prototypes for the several CEOs appearing in the story. The project got me thinking about the many different kinds of extreme leaders I've encountered over the years and how many different ways there are for leaders to fail.

This initial investigation into the subject yielded little background material and even less insight. As a result, I decided to conduct my own "thought experiment," imagining what could happen when behaviors often associated with successful leaders are pushed to the extreme.

Repeated rumination on the subject ultimately yielded a list of ten extreme leadership styles – a collection that describes the behaviors causing the partial or total failure of an executive in his or her job. As you read the descriptions, please note that I've primarily described these defects as "extreme CEO behaviors," as that is where the flaws will be most plainly evident. For the record, the behaviors can apply to anyone in a supervisory position. These behaviors are often less evident below the top managerial level because most supervisors are regularly observed by a superior. CEOs usually aren't.

As a result of this reduced oversight, the behaviors of CEOs are less regulated than the behaviors of those working under them. Who criticizes the CEO to her face? Only the very brave or the very foolish. With a nearly complete lack of constructive criticism, the behavior of the CEO is free to range toward whatever extreme to which she may be naturally inclined.

And, in my experience, this often occurs. In spades.

I've seen most of these failed leadership types in the real world and am (alas) intimately familiar with a few of them:

1. The Super-Critic – In this leadership style, the CEO becomes so critical of everyone's efforts that no one is capable of pleasing her.

2. The Micromanager – Micromanagers take the super critic's behavior one step further, substituting the CEO's judgment for... pretty much everyone's. The Micromanager sees himself as a genius among morons and rarely allows anyone's judgment to stand unaltered.

3. The Burnout – This leader has had enough... of everything – enough struggle, enough competition, and enough conflict. She should retire, but for some reason keeps hanging on, much to everyone's chagrin.

4. The Diva – He really isn't interested in what he can do for the staff or the company, only what they can do for him. The Diva is focused on money, power, prestige, or a combination of all three.

5. The Oddball – Locked into outdated or ineffective leadership paradigms, this CEO's actions are typically disconnected from the ultimate success or failure of the company.

6. The Blame-Gamer – Every problem or shortcoming has a name attached to it, and you can guarantee it isn't his. The Blame-Gamer will make sure to position every risk so that someone else can take the fall.

7. The Procrastinator – Unable to make a decision without perfect information, the Procrastinator is perpetually stuck in neutral. She vainly hopes someone else will step forward and take a stand.

8. The Regurgitator – A variant on the Procrastinator, this leader decides, reconsiders, and then decides again. For subordinates, decision making becomes an endless loop.

9. The Screamer – This CEO "leads" through a cocktail of intimidation, fear, and brow-beating. She is usually dramatic and sometimes reacts just for show – but it definitely doesn't feel that way to those on the receiving end.

10. The Gentleman – He can't imagine doing, saying, or deciding anything in a way that might offend. This CEO has a tough time making decisions that might negatively impact anyone's opinion of him.

This list of extreme leadership types is not exhaustive, nor are the various types an "either/or" proposition. From what I've seen, any given leader may demonstrate characteristics belonging to multiple extreme types while also doing some or even a lot of things right.

The trick in identifying the dominant extreme leadership type in your particular boss is to observe how much time they spend behaving similarly to each of the types described. With a few weeks of casual interaction, most employees have little difficulty recognizing their boss' default "failure mode." With concerted effort, it isn't hard to bring that time down to a few days.

Some types are easy to identify (like the Screamer or the Oddball) while others are a bit more subtle (the Blame-Gamer or the Gentleman). Even though your boss might display elements of more than one type, you should spend most of your effort identifying the dominant style, the one that occupies the greatest portion of his or her bandwidth. That's the style from which most of your problems will come.

For managers trying to get a handle on their own behavioral pitfalls – unfortunately, I must say that self-examination, while perhaps marginally helpful, is unlikely to lead to quick or easy answers. Human beings appear to be constructed in such a way that behavior patterns we readily recognize in others are at least partially hidden from ourselves.

To gain quick, useful insight on your own pitfalls, you're likely to need to talk to someone. Peers can be a helpful (although, often hard to stomach) source of feedback. Former employees may be a better source, particularly if they have nothing to lose by being honest. When all else fails, there are always blind, 360-degree feedback processes that can be utilized. If you decide to go this route, however, make sure to brace yourself – the comments are likely to be brutal. Additionally, if you involve HR, they will likely expect you to "fix" any problems so identified, and to do so quickly.

The following chapters will give you greater insight into each of these extreme leadership types. If you are in doubt as to what a type looks like, the underlying needs that may be driving the behavior, or how the traits tend to play out in real-life management situations, then please read on....

Chapter 2

The Super-Critic

A large part of a manager's daily work consists of dealing with problems, and an important part of that task includes figuring out what went wrong. Digging into past failures can sensitize a manager to the many decisions that caused an issue to arise in the first place. It is a necessary, if unpleasant task.

But criticism is easy to overdo.

In the ideal crucible of critical dissection, and armed with perfect hindsight, many managers become hypercritical.

I remember sitting in MBA classes (taught using the case method and, as a result, heavily focused on classroom discussion) and listening as student after student harshly criticized the actions of real-world managers who were often faced with seemingly insurmountable challenges. My class once had Jack Welch, the now retired CEO of General Electric, visit for a lecture and subsequent Q&A session. Some of my fellow students didn't hesitate before launching into harsh critiques of his management of GE – criticism brazenly offered directly to his face! (Talk about arrogance and overconfidence....) The point being that as managers, we are taught to look for weaknesses and to criticize. It is a practice good for the development of critical thinking skills, but maybe not so good when it comes to handling subordinates.

After two years in this educational environment, one conclusion was crystal clear – it is far easier to criticize the actions of others than to formulate and execute plans yourself. For all the advantages of the case method as a tool of instruction (and there are many), it does seem that this technique firmly sets many a young, budding manager along the path to becoming a Super-Critic.

Main characteristics and variations

The Super-Critic expects perfection and doesn't hesitate to find flaws with everything going on around her. She criticizes how things were done, even if the outcome was respectable. Super-Critics are rarely satisfied with "good" when they can imagine an even better result. If only the Super-Critic had been consulted, allowing her to provide her "piercing insight" and "superior strategy skills" to the situation, things would have clearly turned out even better.

Some Super-Critics learn to toss out the occasional compliment, but these are typically applied only to the most trivial of matters. (*Nice necktie, now on to my critique of your project!*) A few Super-Critics learn to compliment in public and criticize in private, which is slightly easier to stomach, but often still hard to digest.

Another variation of the Super-Critic takes private criticism to a higher level, offering critique only through proxies. This type of Super-Critic has more than a trace of

The Gentleman in them. While the Super-Critic/Gentleman hybrid seems to exert a higher level of control over the urge to criticize, the second-guessing and finger-pointing still flow downhill to the intended target – just through a messenger.

An example

I encountered this last variant in one of my jobs and came to despise the behavior deeply. Not only did I disagree with the notion of criticizing anything and everything – because of the obvious, negative impacts on morale – but I also thought the use of a proxy was particularly cowardly.

In one instance, I was told by another executive that one of my subordinates needed to be replaced by a manager further down in my organization. Not only did I think the conclusion was invalid (the targeted exec was delivering record-setting performance), but I could smell my boss' stink all over the message.

When I confronted her point-blank on this "recommendation," she simply denied it. Eventually, the same message started arriving from other sources. Being an obstinate person, I resisted. Once I left the job for another within the same company, however, my replacement made the switch in a matter of days.

Why they do what they do

The world of the Super-Critic is one of imperfection illuminated by a boss's superior intellect. It is the world of sneering at any job no matter how well done. Undoubtedly, had the Super-Critic lent a direct hand in the job, it would have been done better.

Perhaps the Super-Critic was subject to the same treatment as a child. Perhaps she learned the behavior in an educational institution (like the business school example I previously described). Perhaps by being hyper critical the manager is able to convince herself of her own superiority, thus quelling a subconscious fear.

Or perhaps she is just a perfectionist by nature.

Whatever the underlying psychological driver, the Super-Critic typically advances down her path quite rapidly. Because the core behavior of "criticism" is an accepted and necessary part of daily management, people generally have a tough time identifying where constructive criticism ends and hypercriticism begins. It is difficult, if not completely impossible, to draw such a line accurately, but when you're on the receiving end, you know.

Organizational impacts

Avoidance of criticisms, often by any means available, is one of the principle reactions to the Super-Critic. A Super-Critic's self-boosting ego comes at the expense of the sense of self-worth of their subordinates. Less contact normally represents less exposure to the Super-Critic's caustic, capability-toppling manner. Tougher employees develop protections – a kind of emotional armor – and use that to shrug off the harshest of critical evaluations. Others lose all initiative, realizing that any attempt to go beyond the strict following of the manager's lead invites biting disparagement. And a tendency to tune out the constant stream of criticism can cause team members to miss the portion of the boss's assessment that would have been valuable feedback and improved results.

When the Super-Critic occupies a position high in management, the employee who hears condemnation often wonders about the ultimate source. While harsh judgment often emanates from the CEO Super-Critic herself, occasionally it comes from imitators positioned along the management ladder. Highly placed Super-Critics often inspire other to emulate their behavior. A lead Super-Critic will often express admiration of the quick, piercing disparagement offered by the most aggressive of her subordinates. In such environments, one sometimes hears employees complain that *"nothing is ever good enough,"* or *"the absence of criticism is the only compliment around here."*

Failure mode

The Super-Critic drives talent out of the organization and breaks the drive to achieve in those who remain. When negative critique is all that is offered – regardless of effort or result – most remaining employees reduce their labors to the minimum level necessary to survive. Smart subordinates certainly don't expose themselves to unnecessary risks when the result is almost certain to be a harsh session of second-guessing.

The Super-Critic CEO ultimately fails when the organization can't perform up to expectations. Unfortunately, Boards are not well equipped to detect and remove the Super-Critic based on her caustic effect on subordinates. Instead, Boards normally only see the impact of larger scale problems that result from a loss of talent in the organization. In some companies, this can become evident quickly, while, in a strong franchise with entrenched market positions, it can take a very long time. In fact, hyper-criticism might never become evident to the board in the midst of the daily impact of dozens other factors that influence results.

Under such circumstances, the Super-Critic is there to stay for a long haul.

Coping

As is true with many of the extreme leadership types, the best defense for the victim of the Super-Critic is to leave the company, or at least to leave the Super-Critic's sphere of influence. If you must stay, avoidance and unflinching obedience to the Super-Critic's direction may make the job tolerable – at least for a time.

Longer term, the Super-Critic fails to provide an environment in which the subordinate can make the most of the skills, grow their capabilities, and have a satisfying career.

Chapter 3

The Micromanager

I confess I find it difficult to comprehend this extreme leadership type. While wanting to be in control of "everything" is a fairly common human reaction, micromanagement behavior is so opposed to successful leadership – at least partially because it is so incredibly limiting to the manager, himself – that I'm surprised it exists anywhere but at first-level management. Yet if you look at large organizations, and you can find plenty of Micromanagers distributed throughout the corporate hierarchy.

The term "Micromanager" is loosely thrown around, and it is sometimes misapplied. It's instructive to take a look at specifically what the Micromanager does before we explore what might be making him tick.

Main characteristics and variations
The Micromanager wants to be in control of everything going on in his domain – typically applying little

discrimination between the trivial and the significant. A Micromanager might be manipulating the work on an acquisition in the morning and overruling the selection of dinner napkins in the afternoon. The Micromanager's basic action is one of overriding or supplanting the judgment of others. Often micromanagement is most easily detected by the absence of meaningful delegation.

Micromanagers supersede the judgment and decisions of almost everyone (with the *possible* exception of their corporate superiors). The behavior tends to span almost every action and decision under their command and often extends to anything that might impact their domain in any way. The style tends to be aggressive to the point of domineering (a bully), but I've also seen some Micromanagers who operate with a softer touch. Just because a manager is smiling and speaking calmly doesn't mean he's not a Micromanager.

In my experience, Micromanagers seem to be most common in the lower managerial rungs inside large organizations. This is because a Micromanager tends to run out of bandwidth when his span of control becomes too large.

And yet there are exceptions to this rule.

Most nominally successful Micromanagers learn to disguise some of the most flagrant aspects of their behavior. At a minimum; they find ways to hide it from those above them on the corporate ladder. A Micromanager might be described by their unwitting boss as "details oriented," "on top of their responsibilities," or even "confident."

An example

One senior manager I worked for was a horrible Micromanager, constantly demanding the minutest of details surrounding every decision or recommendation. The environment was frustrating and demeaning, leading to a fairly high rate of turnover.

This particular manager held a staff review every month, where the details of every open issue were critiqued in gory detail. I came to think of the meetings as our "monthly excoriation." In addition to being painfully long, the sessions were guaranteed to result in angry defensiveness and injured feelings.

What was worse, the boss actually "encouraged" (demanded) that we also publically Micromanage one another during the meeting – I suppose in an attempt to make sure no stone was left unturned, no matter how small. Predictably, this led not only to resentment of the boss but resentment of one another. Since subordinates scored points with the boss for well-executed attacks, presenting anything during the meeting was akin to tiptoeing through a minefield. And no matter how carefully reasoned or presented, there was likely to be a battle of some sort.

I can't imagine any strategy more destructive to teamwork than insisting peers openly criticize one another.

Why they do what they do

Fear seems to play into the Micromanager's psychological profile – fear of being wrong or fear of making a mistake. Somewhere in all this there likely is a deep-seated need to be right. I suspect your typical Micromanager is convinced of his own superior abilities and sees others as less capable. It is easier and safer to do things yourself, and if that's not possible, then, at least, you should direct them. Right?

There's probably plenty of insecurity lurking at the bottom of the Micromanager's emotional pool.

Organizational impacts

Micromanagers tend to drive off strong-minded subordinates. What person with a brain and a bit of backbone will tolerate the constant redirection of their efforts? The subordinates that remain under a Micromanager tend to fall in one of three categories – sycophantic toadies, natural followers (who are happy to have the responsibility of decisions making lifted from their shoulders), or those stuck in the organization for a personal reason and forced to grind it out despite the difficult behavior of their leader. The folks in this last category will likely be driven to distraction by the Micromanager, but those in the first two are often completely at home in a micromanaging environment.

Micromanagers negatively impact their organization in several ways. One of these I've already mentioned – they drive off talent. Micromanagers also often make decisions very slowly, acting as the choke point in virtually every process going on within their dominion. If a Micromanager were capable of providing general direction and letting underlings make their own decisions (in other words, of delegating), then a lot more work would occur in the company/ division/ department. And it would likely happen a lot faster.

Perhaps the most subtle impact of micromanagement, however, occurs when subordinates become conditioned to ask "What does the boss want?" rather than "What's right for the business?" I've noticed a tendency for the subordinates of Micromanagers to become greatly preoccupied with "boss trivia" and "boss divining," rather than doing their jobs. They manipulate every process and decision in a vain attempt to give the Micromanager exactly what they think he wants. This can quickly become an exercise akin to rearranging deck chairs on the Titanic. When such behavior is evident, it does not bode well for long-term business performance.

Failure mode

It often requires a mass exodus of subordinates (or the "right" person quitting) to bring this extreme behavior to the attention of superiors. Heaven help you if the Micromanager is the top officer of the company. Barring an attention-grabbing event such as the catastrophic failure of a project, this extreme leadership type can survive in large organizations for an extended period of time, remaining relatively undisturbed.

Coping

Unlike those subordinates cursed with a Super-Critic boss, those dealing with a Micromanager cannot simply avoid him. To a Micromanager, avoidance is equivalent to insubordination. The Micromanager insists on having his finger on every button and directly or indirectly manipulating every decision.

Nope, avoidance as a coping strategy is right out.

I've seen a few subordinates engage in extensive manipulation of their boss in an attempt to get decisions to fall the correct direction. Lobbying those higher in the organization than the boss, selective disclosure of information, soft-pedaling of some major decision elements – all of these actions are both high risk and high effort. But they do work. I suggest the employee stuck under a Micromanager attempt such tactics only on the most critical of decisions.

Beyond the obvious departure from the company and manipulation of the boss, the only other coping strategies I'm familiar with is to "shut up and take it." To "suck it up."

Perhaps a lobotomy would make this approach less stifling.

Chapter 4

The Burnout

Most Burnouts were something else before they slipped into this extreme leadership type. Perhaps the Burnout was once a hard-charging manager on a rapid ascent up the corporate ladder. Or perhaps she was an extreme leader that exhibited another challenging style such as being a Super-critic or a Micromanager.

Then something happened.

Usually, it was an incident that changed everything. An event or epiphany of some kind that vacuumed the interest, enthusiasm and, dare I say, the joy out of the Burnout's work.

This "incident" might have been a personal tragedy, a major career disappointment, or a realization arrived at by observing someone else's sad story. Or possibly the "incident" was merely the accumulation of scores of little disappointments that piled one on top of another – much like that proverbial final straw that cracked the camel's back.

For whatever reason, the Burnout enters a mode where she can no longer care about the company, her co-workers, and particularly she doesn't care about those annoying customers.

Once Burned Out, the afflicted manager normally cannot easily reform.

Main characteristics and variations

The Burnout lacks the necessary motivation to carry out her assigned work. This extreme leader might enthusiastically spend her time doing things that give her energy, but those activities are most definitely not the normal tasks of her job. The Burnout often exhibits habitual fatigue and seems to have a tough time putting on a modest show of interest – even in front of her boss. In an odd moment, she might be caught surfing the web, working a crossword puzzle, or gossiping about peers. The Burnout seems to prefer almost any excuse that allows her to avoid reviewing last month's performance against budget or conducting a staff meeting.

Burnouts are mainly identifiable through their lack of presence and participation. While most are fairly transparent, some learn tricks to disguise their utter absence of motivation – at least in a superficial way. The Burnout tends to be indecisive, uncaring, disengaged and provides little or no inspiration to their team or others in the organization. They go through the motions rather than driving performance (or even providing a reaction, in some instances).

Destructive conflict is often present between subordinates when the Burnout is in charge. Stepping in and settling disagreements is not something the Burnout willingly volunteers to do. Tolerance of a wide range of normally unacceptable behaviors is quite common.

An example

The highest level Burnout I've ever directly observed was once an ambitious, hard-driving executive – until a personal tragedy sucked the energy out of her job. This particular Burnout was able to cruise along as a General Manager for an extended period of time, but only because of an unusual set of circumstances. The core of her business was strong, and at the time the markets were in a steady state – meaning the company was essentially on autopilot, requiring few short-term, day-to-day course adjustments. Eventually and at the right moment, a strong heir apparent stepped in and handled most emerging issues without the formal power of the GM title.

This Burnout eventually retired at a premature age, completely tapped out. I recall her saying, by way of explanation of her early departure, that "she could no longer pretend to care about a tenth of a margin point."

Why they do what they do

As mentioned earlier, most Burnouts have an element of tragedy to their story. Often the tragedy itself helps explain why they are so often allowed to persist in their positions even after their behavior becomes obvious to all. It is often the case that no one has the heart, given what has happened to them, to send the Burnout on her way.

Behind every Burnout I've ever observed was a disaster of some sort – death, divorce, substance abuse, legal problems, etc. The list of potential causes could be as long as one's imagination. Most people process and recover from such events, but the Burnout doesn't seem to be able to do so. In some instances, although recovery is ultimately possible, it happens at such a slow pace that progress is, for all intents and purposes, completely stalled. While compassion for such people is admirable, perhaps companies should be a tad more aggressive in removing Burnouts from the job of supervising others.

Organizational impacts

For subordinates, the Burnout is one of the easiest extreme leadership types to tolerate – mainly because she essentially leaves her direct reports to their own devices. And while such freedom may sound liberating, for many subordinates it isn't ideal. Burnouts certainly won't offer their employees much in the way of helpful guidance on the politics of the organization, nor do they mentor them in any meaningful way – doing so would simply require far too much effort. And while the Burnout is clearly unmotivated, she isn't necessarily willing to accept the blame for failures passively – her own or her subordinates. Employees should never assume that a Burnout won't politically attack them.

Burnouts can also harbor residual behaviors from any of the other extreme leadership types. Or they could have once been a Great Boss – you never know until you explore their behaviors and history more deeply. The lack of motivation tends to mask other tendencies lurking just below the surface, but they can still pop out at unexpected moments.

As a result, subordinates must be prepared for unforeseen reactions from their Burnout boss.

Over time, most Burnouts succeed or fail based on the qualities of their subordinates. And while a Burnout may personally fail on almost every front, a couple of highly capable, well-placed employees can mask their lack of effort.

Failure mode

The Burnout fails because her lack of action becomes obvious to more senior management. Eventually, patience with the Burnout wears thin, despite her personal tragedies that may have previously elicited sympathy. While her superiors may be slow to replace her, usually the Burnout is forced out of the organization when the performance of her group slips. Unless she quits or retires on her own, which is not an infrequent occurrence. A tough business climate or the occupancy of a critical position will likely hasten the forced removal of a Burnout while the opposite set of conditions tends to delay it.

I've never seen a Burnout in the top executive position of a company, but I'm sure it sometimes occurs. In some organizations, a Burnout could conceivably exist at the top for a very long time – if facilitated by the next tier of management, that is. Often the staff below the CEO can "take the ball and run with it" when a chief executive fails to do so.

After a time, such a Burnout will become obvious to even a disengaged board, and when that happens, theoretically the end should rapidly arrive. In practice, boards tend to be cautious and conservative when changing a senior manager. And remember, pulling the trigger on a replacement can take an extended period of time despite any apparent urgency.

Coping

For subordinates, the biggest risk in a Burnout boss is being painted with the same broad brush.

As previously noted, the Burnout is quite likely to be seen by more senior managers as a complacent underperformer, a characterization that is often applied to their team, as well. As such, it is important for the ambitious subordinate to try to separate from the boss in meaningful and obvious ways.

Under ideal circumstances, this would be accomplished through a transfer to a different group or department. When this is impossible, as often proves to be the case, it is of critical importance to make sure others in management are aware of both the limitations placed on individual employees by their disengaged boss and to detail how such employees are successfully contributing despite the added challenges. As one of my old bosses used to say, "she who tooteth not her own horn, will not have her horn tooted."

Such behind-the-scenes self-promotion and politicking may seem distasteful or even improper to some employees, but without it, the risks of having one's contribution tied to the substandard performance of a Burnout boss are quite high.

Under some circumstances, working for a Burnout can actually be an opportunity. In the Burnout's leadership vacuum, sometimes there is room for a subordinate to step up, taking on the lion's share of departmental leadership responsibilities. Showing such initiative can lead to promotion to the position once the Burnout moves on. Of course, this only works if performance is solid, a circumstance that may be difficult to achieve if the Burnout insists on frequently interfering.

Chapter 5

The Diva

Rather than serving the interests of shareholders or other stakeholders, the Diva leader expects the company to revolve around him. We've observed the increase in hiring of "celebrity CEOs" – people with all the right boxes checked and a seemingly unassailable track record – during the 90's and into the new millennium. Celebrity CEOs, if not already Divas, are at least Divas-in-the-making. The typical celebrity CEO arrives on the scene with terrific experience, a gigantic ego, and an attitude that says, "Thank God I've arrived in time to save you all."

Unfortunately, results don't always bear out the high expectations surrounding the arrival of such overly self-confident outsiders into their predictably tough jobs. According to a Harvard Business Review article published in 2006, such appointments result in a short-term pop in stock price, unreasonably high investor expectations, and often ultimately lead to a big disappointment.

In my opinion, at least a part of this can be attributed to the Diva-type behavior that is typical of such executives.

Main characteristics and variations

Divas come in a wide variety of forms – from the high-profile pillar of the community to the self-promoting news hog to a your-purpose-is-to-serve-me egomaniac to the accomplished corporate politician. Diva predilections seem to heighten as a leader approaches the pinnacle job within their organization – that of the CEO. Despite the wide variety of Divas, they share some common characteristics:

- Divas normally focus on "what's in it for me" rather than "how do we all win." This applies to both their own interests as well as how they interpret the actions of others in the organization.
- Divas often neglect internal relationships in favor of external ones, particularly those that they believe can deliver something of value such as new connections, increased fame, or even just some top-shelf ego-stroking.
- Divas think their employees should feel honored to work for them, and they often expect subordinates to bend to every whim and/or treat the Diva like royalty.
- Divas often (but not always) surround themselves with sycophants, who's constant flattery stokes the ego. And they often expect absolute loyalty – to them personally, not to the company – violations of which come with severe consequences.
- Divas generally don't run the organization. They are the outward face of the company and need to be paired with a capable inside manager to make the business function properly. When the Diva is a

CEO, the inside manager is usually either the COO or the CFO.

An example

I had a front row seat (as a peer) for the arrival, struggle, and ultimate failure of a Diva leader at one of my former employers. The executive in question had a stellar background, having worked for a period of time at GE before serving in a high-level job in Asia – an area of the world of great importance to his employing firm.

Unfortunately, he was also a Diva of major proportion. Believing himself to be smarter and better schooled in business than the rest of the management team, he appeared to expect his peers to bend a knee collectively in deference to his superior capabilities.

Not surprisingly, this behavior won him few friends.

Over time, this executive managed to alienate all of his peers with his incessant preening behaviors. When the CEO moved him into the role of heir apparent, people actually began to rebel. Eventually, the boss recognized the Diva was an unsuitable successor, a decision that greatly angered the man. The entire episode ended with our wunderkind Diva leaving the company for greener pastures.

And another

One of my many bosses grew up as a sycophant to a former CEO, and in this role, he bent over backward to treat the CEO as royalty. His job included taking care of every aspect of the CEO's personal comfort, convincing him that he was brilliant, and arranging opportunities for his boss to hob-nob with people in positions of power.

The behavior contributed to (but I suspect didn't create) the man's own Diva-like behaviors.

When the sycophant eventually ascended to a senior management role himself, he expected the same treatment from his subordinates – something he only occasionally received. More than once, I heard him ruminate that the younger generation of managers simply "didn't know how to treat their leaders."

In the case of this leader, his behavior didn't result in organizational or personal failure, but I can assure you it was damned irritating at times! And the lack of compliance to his wishes by various subordinates contributed to a curtailment of their careers on more than one occasion.

Why they do what they do

It is difficult to know for sure what is going on inside a Diva's head. Not being a Diva myself, I've been forced to theorize. I suspect that somewhere deep inside the Diva rests a belief that he doesn't deserve the success he has achieved. Diva behaviors seem to be specifically designed to produce a constant stream of validation from both internal and external sources. It appears that this validation pacifies lingering doubts about the Diva's abilities and worthiness.

Of course, some Divas may simply love the attention and fame/fortune attainable as a business leader, and they engage in a Diva-typical stream of self-promotion simply as a way to grow that attention further. Such a person would be a Diva in their public persona, but in private would likely seem to be much more down-to-earth.

Failure mode

Employees quickly learn that raising praise for their boss' brilliance, rather than delivering anything remotely resembling constructive criticism, is an important survival tactic. Some employees will be confused into thinking that

47

the figurehead, a person who is only superficially involved in the day-to-day operation of the business, actually runs things. Most will eventually learn it's an inside manager (paired with the Diva) that causes the company to perform.

The occasional surreptitiously-delivered eye roll will accompany some of the more outlandish stunts or statements of the Diva, but real critiques will be sparse as they aren't well tolerated. Divas generally do not do well motivating employees over the long term, because their actions and statements have a self-serving undercurrent. Some gifted Divas, however, can manage to "rally the troops" successfully at critical junctures.

Diva behavior is hardest on those closest to such prima donnas. One will often see direct subordinates either transform themselves into sycophantic toadies or leave the company. Once a critical mass of "yes-men" accumulates in senior management roles, the company is vulnerable to wasted resources and even huge strategic blunders. Alas, few if any are willing to challenge the pronouncements of the Diva.

There is a much greater vulnerability if the Diva's "inside person" should depart. Finding a senior executive to be the "yin" to the Diva's "yang" can be quite difficult. During such a transition, the company will be at a heightened level of risk for making bad decisions.

Diva leaders often seem able to continue in their roles for an extended period of time. Since much of the chaos they create surrounds the manner in which they personally benefit from their role as a leader, they don't necessarily make huge errors. And sometimes they really are "that good." Boards are accustomed to dealing with these large egos, particularly since many board members are also Divas and often see nothing unusual or destructive in Diva-ish behavior.

Generally, it requires some type of major business failure to dislodge the Diva from his top executive position.

When the Diva CEO does fail, it is often because of an external faux pas, such as a foolish statement made to the media or some kind of outlandishly selfish behavior that becomes public knowledge. If the Diva is fired, the organization usually gives a collective sigh of relief and then marches on, barely missing a beat. You can bet, however, that all the company insiders will be hoping the next CEO isn't cut from the same cloth.

Coping

If your employer has a "celebrity" CEO that spends most of his time sitting on other boards, is disengaged from day-to-day operations, and can't seem to take criticism, then the chances are good you're dealing with a Diva.

Divas can be hard to stomach, and their frequent insistence on submissiveness and servitude can deal damage to a subordinate's sense of self-worth. As extreme leaders go, however, Divas are one of the easier ones to tolerate.

Avoidance is generally easy with a Diva. Most hob-nob extensively with people outside of the company and are often times more than happy to have their "inside person" deal with whatever issues arise on a daily basis. When you are thrust into the Diva's presence, there is really only one approach that works – deference. If you can't tolerate providing this, you need to look for a new boss/employer.

A word of caution, however, is to never, ever show up a Diva. This can happen in a variety of ways – from successfully executing something that the Diva publically proclaimed "impossible" to uncovering an error or missed opportunity in the Diva's domain. This type of slip up will earn you a quick ticket to somewhere else. It is easier and safer to follow directions, kiss the ring, and never, ever cross your Diva boss.

Given all the damage that can be caused by some of the extreme types of leadership, Divas are relatively benign. And for the employee that can accept a giant ego in their boss, working for a Diva can actually be rewarding.

Chapter 6

The Oddball

I've met several senior leaders that many would consider oddballs. Most of these managers would fall into the classification solely because of their strange appearance traits (dressing as a cowboy, for instance) as opposed to their weird comportment. I have only met a few true Oddballs – leaders where their strange or quirky behaviors materially interfered with the task of managing – and I've never worked for one. Because of my dearth of direct experience, describing the Oddball requires a bit more guesswork than usual – please accept my apologies in advance if a few elements are slightly off.

Main characteristics and variations

The Oddball is sometimes described as an "offbeat" leader – one who often seems to be out of touch with the rest of her management team. Her behaviors can range anywhere from amusingly eccentric to downright bizarre.

Many Oddballs seem to love outdated management fads – remember "Management By Walking Around," "The One-Minute Manager," "Business Process Re-engineering," or "Theory X?" Neither does anyone else. Oddballs seem to latch onto these and other obsolete management theories, ones that have faded into the woodwork.

As a group, Oddballs seem blissfully unaware of how they are seen by others. They often engage in a variety of strange behaviors both in and out of the workplace, seemingly unaware how peculiar everyone finds them. I've seen Oddball behavior primarily in first line supervisors and suspect it is difficult for such a leader to rise much higher in an organization. The ability to read and understand others and knowing how you are viewed are both fundamental to the leadership task, and the Oddball's failure in this area is indicative of a serious limitation.

Oddballs are sometimes superstitious or ritual driven. This variety of Oddball seems to think old and beloved formulas – typically followed to the letter – will inevitably lead to continuing success. This belief is similar to the star athlete who will rub a rabbit's foot before each inning or who always wears her "lucky" green underwear backward for a big game. The managerial equivalent of these rituals can drift so far off track from what's important to the organization that they become more than just a waste of time, instead passing into the category of destructive.

An Example
I recall once meeting an Oddball business owner to discuss the possibility of purchasing her company. When I arrived at her office, I was immediately surprised by the excessive amount of taxidermy. There were dozens of smallish critters (squirrels, possums, raccoons, etc.) mounted in various poses all over her walls. The leader

explained to me how these animals were all "pests" she had shot on the property! Oh, and did I mention that at the time, she was deeply involved in the process of converting her old (and huge) collection of Elvis LP's to digital!

Maybe there was a perfectly good explanation for all of this. A connection to success of the business, however, well....

Needless to say, we never had a second meeting.

Why they do what they do

Oddballs generally appear to be different at their core, and with many their offbeat behaviors worsen with age. They become more eccentric the longer they work and the higher they go in the organization.

I can only hazard a guess as to what might be driving this behavior. A deficiency of some sort in nurture, like a sheltered childhood with limited socialization? Wires crossed in their basic genetics? In some cases, the behaviors are probably clinically definable as some sort of mental illness, although most functional Oddballs undoubtedly fall short of being defined as "impaired."

Failure mode

Those Oddballs that manage to survive successfully in the corporate hierarchy seem to have a tough time separating luck (and luck plays a role in the career of every top manager) from the actions required to drive success. This confusion seems to be at the root of their superstitious, ritualistic behavior. As a result, the Oddball can cause her organization to waste tremendous amounts of energy on practices, systems, analysis, and other elements of their unusual "management mantra" that have little or nothing to do with the organization's success or failure. These practices can range anywhere from annoying (or confusing) to downright success destroying.

Having an Oddball as your leader can also be... well, embarrassing.

Image-conscious executives will keep their distance if for no other reason than to avoid any guilt by association. It can be tough for an Oddball's organization to retain talent when their leader's strange behaviors are plainly visible. The few Oddballs I've met were able to hide their extreme behaviors (sometimes only partially) from superiors – at least for a time. Unfortunately, they appeared to be completely incapable of hiding their peculiarities from subordinates.

Oddballs often fail by driving off or marginalizing their subordinates. Eventually, someone above the Oddball takes notice, and this extreme leader is relieved of her command.

Coping

If you are faced with an Oddball boss, don't lose hope. While some extreme leadership types are tolerated by senior management, Oddballs normally survive because their abnormal behaviors are largely unrecognized.

And while I've seen one or two instances where the Oddball was "delivering the numbers" and thus earned a "pass" from senior management, this was a rare exception. In most cases, the Oddballs' weird actions have a detrimental effect on performance, thus drawing management attention and hastening the end.

Bold employees can speed this along with a few well-documented observations delivered to higher management. In many instances, all it takes if a few stories of bizarre behaviors – corroborated by more than one person – to result in action.

Of course, such initiative is politically risky, and the subordinate is well advised to weigh risk versus reward carefully when engaging in any action that may undermine their boss. Similar political plotting is much less risky (and also less personally beneficial) if the manager is not in the employee's direct chain of command. And since most Oddballs are relatively harmless (other than being annoying) plotting against them will typically be a risk not worth taking, particularly as it brands you as disloyal in the minds of others.

The employee who is cursed with an Oddball as their CEO has a much more difficult problem. CEOs (and owners) tend to have orders of magnitude greater latitude than other managers. Unless the business falls on hard times, an Oddball CEO is likely not going anywhere anytime soon.

Under such circumstances, the employee must either embrace their Oddball leader's behaviors or search for a job elsewhere.

Chapter 7

The Blame-Gamer

We'd like to think corporate success – and success in life, in general – is based much more on the check marks in our "win" column than anything else. People call such environments "meritocracies," implying that those demonstrating merits are rewarded.

Unfortunately, meritocracy is often little more than an elusive myth. Sometimes avoiding the taking of responsibility for mistakes becomes as important than any successes. This is the environment that encourages the emergence of the Blame-Gamer.

There is an ugly aspect of human nature – one that encourages us to zero in on mistakes, failures, and losses, no matter how few and far between. Most of us take greater notice of the foibles and pitfalls of others than their positives. We search for, discover, and dwell on shortcomings of every kind. This is why the often discussed "Positive Work Environment" is a seldom achieved ideal – because it goes against our internal wiring.

This tendency causes failure to loom much larger than success in the eyes of most – including most bosses and other important senior employees. Sometimes it is a lack of failures, rather than a list of successes, that determines where your career goes.

The Blame-Gamer understands this element of human nature very well and is prepared to take advantage of it.

Main characteristics and variations

Blame-gaming is what is sarcastically described in management circles as "the search for the guilty and the punishment of the innocent." To the Blame-Gamer, every problem, failure, or shortcoming has a name associated with it – someone who is "guilty." And believe me, the guilty party is not someone the Blame-Gamer is trying to identify to offer encouragement, advice, or constructive criticism.

One of the things Blame-Gamers rarely seem to do is to take the time to understand the circumstances surrounding a failure. Was the original strategy sound? Were there environmental factors making success impossible to achieve? Were the expectations of a successful outcome reasonable? To the Blame-Gamer, such questions are irrelevant. In his world, examining such factors is called "excuse making," and it interferes with the search for the person or persons responsible for screwing things up.

The worst variety of Blame-Gamer has his own name, the Scapegoater. This creature (who shares this moniker with the most destructive and heinous of political tactics, as described in my book, *Navigating Corporate Politics*) takes blaming to a new level by lining up victims to take the blame for any and every risky project falling under his responsibility. It isn't much of a leap from "searching for the guilty" to "throwing the innocent under the bus."

An example

Not every acquisition goes according to plan, and a few actually turn into major challenges. I was faced with one such acquisition soon after arriving in one of my general management jobs.

The deal had been completed by my predecessor, but the former owner of the business decided to retire on my watch. With the help of one of my subordinates (who had direct responsibility for the acquired business), I hired a GM to run the place.

We made a bad choice. The new General Manager, an excellent sales and marketing executive, had no idea how to handle operations. He piled multiple bad decisions on top of one another, quickly drove a marginally profitable business into the red.

My Blame-Gamer boss immediately pointed the finger at the new GM. In my boss' mind, the problem was the person, and the solution was simple – get rid of him. My subordinate didn't agree, feeling that with the right help, the operational issues could be resolved, and we could still gain great advantages from the GM's sales experience. Was the GM flawed? Sure, just like every other human being. Did he need to be fired? My subordinate and I agreed the answer to this was "no."

But when the GM wasn't immediately terminating, the Blame-Gamer began pointing the finger at my subordinate. "He's also a problem," I heard repeatedly. When I wouldn't fire them both, I eventually ended up in his sights, as well. For this boss, it was important to be able to attach a name to every problem and then eradicate the problem much as a tumor was incised by a surgeon.

This incident was a part of the reason I was eventually released from that job.

Why they do what they do

Blame-Gamers seem to believe that every business problem can be successfully resolved by a person of sufficient talent. When a failure occurs, to the Blame-Gamer it must surely be due to a defect in the person charged with implementation or execution. Rarely are flawed strategies or unwinnable circumstances accepted as viable explanations for failure.

In many cases, the behavior can be more sinister. Blame-gaming is often a brazen attempt to divert attention away from the Blame-Gamer, himself, by offering up another employee as a sacrifice. This tactic is known as "Scapegoating" and is a mere hop, skip and jump beyond simply searching for "the guilty."

At the root of the Blame-Gamer's behavior, there appear to be two incorrect assumptions – that all externalities can be overcome by a person of sufficient talent and that the Blame-Gamer's own work cannot possibly be the cause of any problem. This latter assumption undoubtedly has something to do with deeply seated insecurity and the need to establish one's own presupposed superiority over others.

Failure mode

The impact on the organization is fairly predictable – rampant conservatism. In the Blame-Gamer environment, where every "failure" is punished far more than any "success" is ever celebrated, it pays to avoid taking risks. With a Blame-Gamer in control, most employees are reluctant to bring forward ideas unless they're pretty much a sure thing. Clever subordinates strive for recognition by presenting ideas for new projects or improvement projects but then shy away from involving themselves in any aspect of the implementation. Goals and targets, which the wise employee already tries to set as low as possible, will be pushed even lower in a Blame-Gamer environment where there is little upside to agreeing to anything beyond the easiest objectives.

Ferreting out overly risk-averse groups within a large corporation can be extremely difficult, thus creating an environment that allows the Blame-Gamer to persist in his position for an extended period of time. Even if this symptom is identified, the Blame-Gamer is in the perfect position to lay this problem at the feet of one of his hapless subordinates. If you work for a Blame-Gamer, chances are good he'll hang in there for a long, long time, not bold enough to merit promotion, but never being tagged with responsibility for any failures.

The company ruled long enough by a Blame-Gamer can sometimes be overtaken by smaller, less risk-averse competitors – those willing to experiment with innovative new systems, products, and processes. The Blame-Gamer-led firm will be slow to move on new ideas, as employees are aware they are on the hook for producing anything less than stellar success.

Coping
Coping with the Blame-Gamer is relatively simple – don't take unnecessary risks resulting in unnecessary exposure. When backed into a corner and forced into accepting a role in the implementation of a questionable project or initiative, make sure to identify failure risks and externalities early and loudly. Sure, it might make you sound a bit like Chicken Little, but better to sound the alarm repeatedly that the sky is falling than to have it fall on you!

The unfortunate side-effect of following this advice is that while you might save your job, you're unlikely to advance – particularly as your Blame-Gamer probably isn't going anywhere anytime soon. If you're not content with this, taking some calculated risks might make sense, as long as you're fully aware you may be betting your job on them.

Moreover, when a Scapegoater is active (the Blame-Gamer who is lining up targets for potential failures for his own self-preservation or even for his own advancement), there will be times when avoiding fault becomes impossible. Of course, the best protection against this inevitability is to make sure your projects are always successful. When this is not possible, a well-timed exit from the department, division, or company can keep your reputation and future intact.

Alas, if you don't take the initiative when you fall in the Blame-Gamer's sights, you're likely to end up with severe career damage or even on the street looking for a job – and there will be a gigantic skid mark on your resume.

Chapter 8

The Procrastinator

With the Procrastinator, being able to gather enough data to make a decision is a real problem. Procrastinators have difficulty making decisions, and once they finally do manage to move forward, their subordinates discover that new information can reopen seemingly closed issues (see Chapter 9 on the Regurgitator). With the Procrastinator, there is a risk of decisions being strung out forever, effectively preventing forward progress within the organization.

The typical time arc for a project in the Procrastinator's organization could include any and all of the following: an initial review, multiple demands for more data, a series of further reviews – each with no clear decision, vague direction that becomes slightly more clear as the process progresses (although often different from the original direction, and rarely definitive), no ultimate closure prior to the start of implementation, and plenty of hand-wringing after the fact.

And yes, it drives her subordinates to distraction.

Main characteristics and variations

Procrastinators delay making decisions, wish for additional data that is either impractical or impossible to obtain, and sometimes perform flip-flops in direction. If a Procrastinator can find a reason to put off today's decision until tomorrow, she will take it – unless she can delay for even longer.

Procrastinators have difficulty committing and are particularly helpless when a situation lacks perfect information – perfect rarely being available in the real world. When the situation is ambiguous, the Procrastinator often relies on the whims and opinions of those above her in the organizational hierarchy (often a board member, if the Procrastinator is the CEO). Unfortunately, "higher ups" regularly lack a clear perspective on the situation and often tend to substitute tried-and-true "rules of thumb" for direct knowledge when forming their opinions. This happens because identifying similarities to past experiences is a lot easier and a lot faster than spending the time and effort needed to understand a unique situation thoroughly. If and when the Procrastinator finally does take a stand, she often errs on the side of conservatism, killing off potentially valuable new ideas or concepts.

From a subordinate's perspective, any project or initiative must run a gauntlet of painful reviews, where at any stage a small bit of data pointing toward the "no-go" solution will spell the project's ultimate demise. Keeping projects alive often requires subordinates to selectively present data or to avoid the Procrastinator to the greatest degree possible.

An example

I once worked for such a Procrastinator, and her inability to make a decision drove me to distraction. In one particular decision – a "go, no-go" call for an acquisition – I literally went back to the sellers FOUR TIMES to renegotiate elements of the contract. Each of these renegotiations occurred because some new concern would pop into my boss' head. With each cycle, she would convince herself that the subject of the concern represented a fatal flaw in the deal, and only further concessions by the sellers or detailed contractual protections could put these worries to rest.

After the fourth renegotiation, I simply let the project die the death that was undoubtedly destined from the outset.

As an interesting side note, the primary criticism of this manager by her superiors was that she was unable to put to use the horde of cash the company had accumulated. From the inside of the organization, the reason for this behavior was crystal clear – she simply couldn't commit!

Why they do what they do

At the core of the Procrastinator's indecisiveness is the manifestation of a fear of making a mistake. Anyone that has spent time in a large corporation can verify that managerial failures are generally punished far more than any successes are rewarded. The Procrastinator attempts to hang onto the option forever of pulling the plug on any (remotely) controversial or risky project.

Procrastination, in its essence, is a vain attempt to have one's cake and eat it, too.

Failure mode

Employees typically find this extreme leadership style provides no support for their work. In an environment ruled by a Procrastinator, it is difficult to build upon past successes, as past decisions never seem to be fully settled.

Subordinates may also find themselves spending enormous amounts of time searching for confirming facts and figures that simply don't exist or cannot be distilled.

Managerial sponsors of projects constantly find themselves trying to control the revelation of data to the Procrastinator and defending their past work. This preoccupation definitely reduces the effort spent on proposing actions that will advance the company. The Procrastinator's organization is one where managers spend an inordinate amount of energy trying to hold onto meager gains.

Valiant managers tend to "ask for forgiveness rather than permission," putting their careers in high-risk situations on a regular basis by moving forward with plans before their leader has ruled. Eventually, the company's most innovative leaders become frustrated and search for jobs elsewhere.

In her quest for "perfect information," Procrastinators tend to demand extensive proof to back up nearly every step in the decision-making process – even ones that might seem obvious to others. Constant mining for unnecessary data drains the organization of energy and also contributes to a general "analysis paralysis," slowing down nearly everything.

Ultimately the organization stagnates and then calcifies. Fairly obvious decisions are left dangling, and far too many projects are rejected. The organization becomes focused on divining what it takes to obtain the approval of the leader rather than focusing on what is right for the business. Innovation is stifled, and progress in the organization becomes limited to what the Procrastinator herself is personally willing to approve.

The organization can persist in this state for quite a time, particularly if the industry is mature, competitors are slow to change, and there are no disruptive technologies nipping at the firm's heels. When the end of the Procrastinator's reign finally does arrive, the company is often woefully behind competitors and in need of substantial catching up. This typically requires self-starting managers to seize the initiative – the exact type of employee that has likely fled the company in frustration during the Procrastinator's rule.

Coping

Some Procrastinators will allow subordinates to continue to run projects as long as she has "plausible deniability" – in other words as long as blame for any mistakes will fall to the subordinate rather than the boss. An ambitious employee can sometimes successfully drive their own careers forward when working for this flavor of Procrastinator, although the opportunity comes at great personal risk. After all, when something goes wrong, most of us want a boss in our corner to act as an advocate. But in my experience, this type of Procrastinator is relatively rare.

More common is the Procrastinator who will insist on putting her hands on everything happening within her area of responsibility, looking a bit like a very indecisive Micromanager. Here, the subordinate has only two options – defy the boss and hope to justify such behavior to those higher up (an extremely risky proposition) or accept the process for what it is – slow, annoying, and often a major waste of effort.

If the Procrastinator has any "silver lining" as an extreme leader, it is that she is often sidelined fairly early in her managerial career. While bosses often don't understand the dynamics of what is going on in a subordinate's department, they can usually spot a lack of output. Once a track record of under-delivering is on the radar screen, the Procrastinator's days are normally numbered.

Those Procrastinators that do survive typically do so by jumping assignments or jobs fairly often. In most cases, I recommend that a Procrastinator's subordinates simply hold their breath and hope that they won't be plagued with this extreme leader for very long.

And while the option always exists to "blow the whistle" on a Procrastinator boss, I would advise against it. The Procrastinator's behavior, when examined in small doses, can look quite reasonable to others. It is only when the totality of the leadership style is explored that the inefficiency and waste become obvious.

Chapter 9

The Regurgitator

The Regurgitator is similar to the Procrastinator in several ways but maintains one notable difference – the Regurgitator is NOT afraid to make a decision. Making the call is never the issue with this extreme leadership style. Sticking with it is.

The Regurgitator loves to dredge up old decisions and endlessly rehash them. This extreme leadership style is characterized by numerous flip-flops, each of which comes with a degree of certainty that makes it *appear* to be final.

Until it isn't.

Main characteristics and variations

Most Regurgitators seem decisive and self-confident on the surface. They deal with ambiguity much better than the Procrastinator and are willing to make decisions based on the information available at the time.

But they can't seem to move past it.

The Regurgitator typically reconsiders old decisions when any new piece of information come to light or when any new opinion is vocalized by someone in a position of authority. This latter type of Regurgitator, a politician at heart, is the most capricious of these two main types. The political Regurgitator listens to good advice from above, but also factors in whims, biases, and uninformed opinions into the equation of nearly every decision. When those opinions change or vary (or when someone even higher in the food chain expresses a conflicting viewpoint), the decision is pulled out of the "finished" pile, retooled, and sometimes even completely reversed. Of course, it doesn't seem to matter if the implementation has already begun!

And while reconsidering a major decision isn't always a bad thing, Regurgitators of both types typically take re-evaluation to an extreme.

An example

I once worked with a Regurgitator who drove everyone in his business unit bananas. Nothing was ever final until some irreversible "point of no return" was reached (such as a payment being made for a purchase or an employee's promotion being publically announced). Even then there were occasionally times when he attempted to claw back such decisions – particularly if a board member expressed a contrary opinion. Employees working in this environment watched as their competitors and peers in other departments passed them by – despite the fact that they were paddling as fast and hard as they could. While they labored to succeed, their boss remained fixated on reconsidering every element of every improvement project, revising details of the business's value proposition, and even flip-flopping on how the accounting was handled. A coworker once described the environment as "trying to sprint through quicksand."

In one instance, I found myself re-re-evaluating the location of a new production plant after the facility lease had already been signed and building modifications were well underway!

As it turned out, there was good reason to have doubts about that particular location decision – the financial projections for the project had serious flaws and almost certainly should never have been approved in the first place. The problem, however, was not with the building selected, but instead with some of the overly optimistic assumptions built into the financial model for the project. Just because the hand-wringing was over the wrong aspect of the project didn't mean the process to which we were subjected was any less painful. In fact, in the end, the rabbit trails I was forced to run down actually made matters worse, a result of the additional delay.

But such is the stock and trade of a Regurgitator – reconsidering both those aspects of a decision that are important as well as those that are insignificant, thus keeping the future constantly in flux.

In what has been a singular event in my career, that particular Regurgitator actually realized he was damaging the business with his extreme leadership style and brought in a subordinate to handle ordinary, day-to-day decisions. Even afterward he sometimes couldn't seem to stop himself, often meddling in and reversing trivial decisions much to everyone's chagrin.

Why they do what they do
Unlike the Procrastinator, who seems to have a deeply rooted fear of making the wrong choice, the Regurgitator never seems to lack the self-confidence to make a call –

only to stick by it. When any odd bit of data or opinion seems to call into question a judgment already long put to rest, rather than brush off the contradiction as "too little too late," the Regurgitator attempts to revisit decisions even at the risk of negating already completed work. There might be a little perfectionism thrown in here – as in searching for a flawless decision regardless of the downstream consequences. The behavior might also have the noblest of motives, to make the "best" decision possible, but simply neglects to take into account the temporal aspects of the here and now. I used to observe this many years ago when in the automotive business, executives making late-stage styling changes on a vehicle that had cascading effects through the car's major mechanical systems. Project teams used to cringe when a senior executive requested a project review.

For many Regurgitators, as I previously noted, corporate politics also has a role to play in their behavior. Some of the most egregious Regurgitators are deft politicians that are always measuring which way the wind is blowing before and after taking a step forward. Unlike a natural Regurgitator, who is attempting to optimize, the political Regurgitator is likely to add another layer of confusion to the situation. His demands to reconsider and change direction will often seem completely inexplicable to subordinates.

Failure mode

Regurgitators waste tremendous amounts of resources – perhaps even more than Procrastinators. Where a Procrastinator will demand endless streams of data to support tentative conclusions, Regurgitators sometimes demolish partially completed work. Not only does every late-stage reconsideration of a project introduce waste and delay, but it also has a negative impact on morale.

As in the Procrastinator's organization, a Regurgitator's mismanagement will typically take a long time to become evident to superiors. Regurgitators are usually quite skilled at justifying their flip-flopping, often successfully convincing superiors that as a result of their "diligence" a major error has been avoided. Alas, Regurgitators don't appear to be any better at making the correct call than the average manager despite their frequent course corrections. (The above example on the factory location is a prime example of this.) Without measurably better decisions, all the course reversals ultimately lead to less productivity within the unit. While senior managers may never discover the impacts the Regurgitator has on subordinates, over the long haul they can usually see that output in his area is substandard.

During a lengthy tenure, forward progress slows substantially as the organization takes two steps back for every three taken forward. Over time, the organization stagnates. As is true with most of the extreme leadership styles, capable subordinates with options will leave, eventually creating a talent drain which may take years to overcome.

Coping

For subordinates, Regurgitation looks like the leadership equivalent of resetting a video game every time a possible mistake has been made – the issue becomes how do you ever progress beyond the first level? The organization becomes forever locked in an endless "Groundhog Day" loop, repeatedly re-evaluating basic management principles and the simplest of decisions.

Subordinates in the organization usually compensate for this style by trying to avoid involving the Regurgitator whenever possible. Attempting to keep decisions out of the Regurgitator's hands usually means that subordinates must either take on greater risks themselves or go over the Regurgitator's head whenever the option exists. This strategy comes with obvious inherent risk.

Many subordinates eventually accept the constant reprocessing of old decisions as a matter of course within the organization, rolling their eyes and then simply slogging onward. When enough subordinates accept Regurgitation as the norm, it can easily become ingrained in normal business systems and practices, and it becomes extremely difficult to root out. Employees that find themselves in such an environment should guard against the acceptance of such thinking.

Chapter 10

The Screamer

I walked into the conference room, sliding along the back wall so as not to disturb the presentation underway. It took me a few moments to notice that every eye was fixed on a woman standing among the audience. I studied her closely, noticing the bulging veins in her neck, the hands clenched into fists at her side, her face a deep shade of scarlet.

Then I realize she is locked in a "battle to the death" with the presenter, a man who looks like a terrified rabbit hoping that the safety of his hole is somewhere nearby and that he'll soon be given an opportunity to escape.

Seconds later, the audience member – the company's CEO, as it turned out – let loose with a torrent of expletives delivered at such volume I could swear loose pens and pencils vibrated on the tables.

This was my first introduction to the Screamer.

Main characteristics and variations

The Screamer is the alpha wolf of her corporate pack, and if you don't acknowledge that within the first fifteen minutes of meeting her, it's probably because you're deaf. Screamers come in a large variety of styles – yellers, cursers, table-pounders, etc. I once met a Screamer that would actually throw things at people. Interestingly, I've never encountered a female Screamer (despite ironically utilizing female pronouns in this particular chapter) although I'm sure they're out there.

The Screamer usually gives the impression she is a hot-head, and sometimes the truth is that simple. The out-of-control, bad-tempered Screamer deserves limited attention in our treatment of this extreme leadership types for a simple reason – she rarely survives to middle management and almost never makes it to a senior executive position. If you're working for a Screamer that simply can't control her temper, you should probably get out. As soon as possible. No matter how many apologies (which are quite rare), vows to change, or counseling sessions are undertaken, it is highly unlikely that the Screamer's basic raging temper is going to change. As the old saying goes: "A tiger can't change its stripes."

Some Screamers, however, are much more deliberate, harnessing white-hot anger to probe, test, and challenge anyone and everyone in the organization. Of the Screamers I've met, it is only this second type that seems able to ascend into upper levels of the corporate hierarchy. Boards often appear to see such leaders as "*strong*" or "*demanding*," as opposed to "*out of control*" and "*a risk.*"

An example

I once worked under a notable Screamer (the one I described in this chapter's introduction), and although I didn't report directly to her, nor did I often find myself on the receiving end of her vitriol, she set the tone for the entire company. One telling incident gave me insight into the method behind her apparent madness.

During a dry run for a large management-group presentation, the Screamer stopped the presenter mid-sentence and demanded that he "back up to that slide with the numbers." She had detected a contradiction between the data presented and the explanation the senior executive standing in the front of the room was wrapping around it. I saw the CEO's face begin to redden as she studied the slide. Then she issued a loud, angry challenge to the exec.

Normally this was where managers began to fold, either attempting to explain what they were trying to say or just standing in silence and hoping the eruption would soon be over (not a good strategy with this particular screamer, as I later learned). Not this particular executive/victim. Instead, he fired back at the CEO with more emotional energy than he'd received, accusing the boss of intentionally misinterpreting his strategy.

Louder "disagreement" was exchanged on both sides, and then the executive really lost it. He was almost foaming at the mouth. I heard the CEO say in a calmer, quieter voice, "Stop it! Stop it! Stop it! You're embarrassing me, and you're embarrassing yourself."

That abruptly halted the outburst, and both of them glared at one other for a moment. Moments later, the CEO sat down, and the executive finished his presentation as if nothing had happened. A few minutes after the meeting concluded, I saw them in the hallway, laughing about something.

It was at that point I realized the CEO's screaming was 90% act and only 10% emotion, an observation that held true at least most of the time. Based on the initial reaction, I'm sure it didn't feel that way to the executive on the receiving end of a tirade.

The CEO's method was deliberately provocative, intentionally testing the metal of the person on the receiving end.

Honestly, all I could think was, "what a crappy way to treat your people."

Why they do what they do

The type of Screamer described in the above example expect subordinates to "stand up to the boss" and "fight back." From the perspective of the average subordinate, however, a raging boss looks like a lion roaring and licking her chops just prior to the kill. It's a rare person indeed who will go toe-to-toe with a lion. The underlying assumption by the Screamer is that only "the best people" will actually stand up to her. Failing the test, the weaker ones are encouraged to move voluntarily to another job or a different organization. The fallacy of this method is assuming that an employee with exceptional courage is somehow better at their job than a person who might be more reserved.

Or perhaps the Screamer is simply confused, thinking that raised voices and table pounding are what leadership is all about. While I've not personally experienced this type of Screamer, I understand they lurk in some companies, appearing to be reasonable bosses until some disaster occurs and they shift into attack mode.

Garden-variety Screamers are exactly what they seem to be – unfettered, ill-tempered bullies. Challenge them and they'll likely come back at you with both barrels. This type of Screamer is not looking to test your metal. She's after simple, unopposed compliance

Telling the difference between these two types of Screamers is nearly impossible without careful and repeated observation of them in action – something that most employees simply don't achieve before finding themselves in the Screamer's sights.

Screamers of either type seem to subscribe to a form of social Darwinism (where only the strong survive) or simply feel it is better to be feared than liked or respected. This latter viewpoint seems to have some merit. I've known employees working for Screamers that put out amazing volumes of production (more emphasis on quantity rather than quality) when the Screamer is riding them.

Failure mode

In smaller organizations, it is rare to find more than one Screamer. Being the alpha wolf in such an organization includes the expenditure of great effort to make sure no one else challenges the Screamer's leadership position.

In larger organizations, a curious thing appears to happen. I've seen the alpha wolf allow a few younger, potential alphas to stick around. Perhaps the motive is simply flattery – imitation being, perhaps, its sincerest form. It is also possible the decision is more deliberate – perhaps having its roots in succession planning. Whatever the reason, the typical Screamer appears to see the continuation of her behavior as an essential part of ongoing organizational success.

The balance of the organization is often sheltered from the Screamer (often by being buried well below her in the organization), or else they live in nearly constant terror of every encounter. Exposure to this leader is definitely seen as both a blessing (an opportunity to stand out) and a curse (the risk of being crushed under heel). It is a situation not typically sought by most of the management team.

In cases where the Screamer is in place for an extended period of time, a collection of "soothsayers" sometimes develops within the managerial ranks. These are employees who attempt to inform others what the boss *really* wants. Soothsayers create a lot of useless busy work and can waste enormous amounts of the company's efforts.

Since the ability to survive an emotionally charged battle is NOT normally a key to success for most corporate jobs, there is typically a high rate of unnecessary turnover in a Screamer-led organization. If the company develops a strong enough reputation for this management style, recruiting may suffer as well. The behavior also tends to result in a shortage of qualified employees, and many of those forced to remain may find themselves overworked and wondering why they stick around. The Screamer can generate risk aversion like no other extreme, resulting in an organization that becomes regimented, calcified, and inflexible.

Screamers seem to do fairly well overall when compared to the other extreme leadership styles. This may be due to the motivational power of the fear they spread. There seem to be quite a few Screamers in positions of high authority, and their companies seem to suffer less than the organizations of many of the other extreme leaders. Still, the Screamer would be the last extreme leader I would personally want for a boss.

I'm sure many others feel the same.

Coping
Those employees foolish enough to attempt to appease the Screamer will almost certainly be disappointed. By attempting placation, subordinates classify themselves as

"lambs," and we all know what lions do to lambs. This is exactly the kind of employee the Screamer is either consciously or unconsciously trying to drive out of the company.

Standing up to the Screamer is a better strategy, but only when the behavior is largely an act. Going toe-to-toe with the boss is almost certain suicide if the Screamer is simply an out-of-control bully.

Most people stuck in an organization with a Screamer will try to avoid this extreme leader. Where avoidance is possible, it can at least reduce anxiety. Avoidance also often becomes a barrier to advancing, as moving up almost always requires extensive exposure to the boss.

The best coping strategy for many is to simply bide their time and look for something in a company more compatible with their own needs and personal style.

Even better is simply avoiding this kind of boss from the start. While many extreme leadership types are subtle and challenging to identify during the hiring process, a little research and few pointed questions ought to tip you off to the fact that your potential boss is a Screamer.

Chapter 11

The Gentleman

Nearly everyone likes the Gentleman – at least in the beginning. This extreme leader is exceedingly image-conscious and is agreeable, affable, and gets along easily. The Gentleman (or Gentlewoman if he is a she) tends to agree with everyone he talks to, fully aware there is little that strokes an ego more than the implicit approval of a person in a position of power.

You can spot the Gentleman from a mile away – he's the leader that privately agrees with almost every wild utterance but sits silently when the same discussion happens in front of others. He is easy on the ego and an entertaining dinner companion.

The problem with the Gentleman is you can't trust anything he says.

Main characteristics and variations

The Gentleman is invariably ingratiating, a behavior which is essential to developing and nurturing a positive image. He tends to straddle controversial issues, not wanting to take sides, as doing so may lead to a tarnishing of his all-important reputation.

In fact, the safeguarding of perceptions about the Gentleman's character becomes an end unto itself.

The Gentleman is particularly sensitive to how he looks in the eyes of subordinates, suppliers, shareholders, and other corporate stakeholders. This sensitivity substantially impacts how he makes decisions. Being a Gentleman generally means ignoring conflict, avoiding blatant politicking, and sometimes even ducking simple disagreements. "Avoidance" is the Gentleman's watchword.

But it's the lack of transparency that causes this otherwise largely benign leadership style to become problematic. When subordinates don't know where they stand, they make errors, engage in pointless battles, and waste tremendous amounts of effort. With a Gentleman for a boss, you rarely receive honest feedback.

An example

Of all the extreme leadership styles, falling into this one has always been my greatest personal danger. Since I have a deeply-rooted need to be "liked," I've often found myself tempted to shy away from difficult or messy situations. It takes a concerted, conscious effort to make tough decisions when doing so might result in making enemies or fueling detractors. Avoiding becoming the Gentleman required me to be on the lookout constantly for situations where I would be tempted to take the easy path and to instead focus on doing what was right.

One area where this played out was with performance appraisals. What I was tempted to do was to handle these evaluations the same way I've seen many other Gentleman managers do it – burying important criticisms in the midst of a mountain of praise and verbally soft-pedaling whatever limited critique I planned to offer.

Resisting this urge, I developed my own appraisal method which I call the "elevator" appraisal. In an elevator appraisal, I intentionally limited praise to only two or three items while making sure to devote most of our discussion to whatever might be holding back the employee. Were these appraisals fun? No, but I needed such a tool to prevent myself from sliding into Gentleman mode. Gentleman appraisals would have been a lot softer and nicer, like a pre-warmed bathrobe. The problem with them is they wouldn't tell the employee what he or she needed to know.

Some general advice if you find yourself falling into a Gentleman leadership pattern – run to the problem, not away from it. Doing so will ensure that the most critical issues aren't swept aside in an attempt to "be nice."

And another one

One of my Gentleman bosses once decided he wanted me to fire one of my subordinates. Being a Gentleman, he couldn't just sit down and discuss the situation with me – that would be far too much risk to his well-cultivated image as our corporate "Mr. Nice-Guy." Instead, he used a surrogate, another senior manager, to make sure I got the message. That exec hinted around at what the boss wanted without ever providing any direct attribution back to the prime mover of the decision.

My basic problem was simple – the Gentleman didn't want me to know he was behind the move to terminate the employee. He wanted me to come to the same conclusion as he had without his direct involvement,

Being a bit obstinate, I ignored the hints. I valued the employee in question and decided I wasn't about to make a move unless I was directly ordered to do so – hints be damned. More intimations arrived from new surrogates, each offering a slightly different version of the same rationale, and all came to the same conclusion – dump the manager. Eventually, this became quite wearing, and I decided to confront the Gentleman.

The results of the conversation were predictable.

"I understand you don't like Ms. X in the VP of Sales job. Why do you want me to get rid of her?" I asked.

"I never said that," the Gentleman replied. "No, not at all. I like Ms. X."

No matter how much I probed, the Gentleman was not going to take ownership of the recommendation. What could I do? Call him a liar?

Eventually, the hints grew into "counsel" and ultimately morphed into "blunt advice." I stuck to my guns, however. Eventually, I was removed from that job (a promotion, of sorts) and in a few short weeks, Ms. X was given her walking papers.

Apparently my replacement listened a lot better than I!

Why they do what they do

At his core, the Gentleman has a desperate desire to be liked by everyone while nurturing the self-serving belief that by being liked he will be more effective. I've most often witnessed Gentleman leaders-in-the-making among the salesperson ranks, where making tough decisions that might potentially anger customers – no matter how wrong or unreasonable they are – has little to no upside. Some respond to this situation by taking the customer's side and fighting against internal interests. The future Gentleman tries to search for a compromise where everyone will be happy.

In addition to the need to be liked (or loved, or adored), some Gentlemen have a deeply rooted abhorrence of conflict. This manifests in a strong need to avoid any possible situation where a skirmish may erupt. A telltale sign you are dealing with a Gentleman-in-residence is the absence of any conflict-laden or emotionally charged events.

The Gentleman can seldom give effective critiques or intervene in conflicts, often allowing small problems or irritations between subordinates to grow to the point where they become major issues. I've seen Gentleman leaders continue to smile and joke about skirmishes until issues went well past nuclear melt-down in severity. At that point, some Gentleman leaders may react severely, releasing a dam-break of pent up stress, and leaving the target of their anger both surprised and confused.

Failure mode

The conflict between organizational peers is often permitted to simmer and escalate under the Gentlemen's managerial hand. As the Gentleman avoids intervening to drive issues to a conclusion, problems simmer, and tensions grow. In such cases, it isn't at all unusual for the Gentleman to use a proxy or some other circuitous route to make his true wishes known.

Most people in the organization find this extreme leader to be a likable sort – particularly when they don't have to deal with some of his behavioral eccentricities. If the Gentleman is the CEO, most of the burden of any corporate dirty work falls on those subordinates near the top. This often times results in substantial conflict, politicking, and buckets full of ambiguity near the apex of the managerial ranks.

The biggest negative impact on the company of the Gentleman is wasted effort. Organizations headed by Gentlemen devote large amounts of time to wasteful political battles and, in the absence of clear direction or feedback, to confused second guessing. There can also be substantial turnover of top management as executives become frustrated by their leader's ambiguity and lack of transparency. The Gentleman, however, often has little trouble replacing these departing executives – his apparent abundance of soft-spoken kindness acts as a siren's song to potential new recruits. The underlying challenges of working within a Gentleman-led organization are rarely apparent during the short time of an interview.

Of all the extreme types, the Gentleman's organization may have the greatest chance of long-term success. Typically, this comes at a steep price for those working directly for him.

Coping

Dealing with the Gentleman is a guessing game. While such a leader is often liked and admired by those some distance from his inner circle, those who directly work for the Gentleman often find their standing to be unclear.

In such a situation, developing informal communication channels within the organization is mandatory to survival. If an employee is uncertain what the boss wants and where the dividing line might lie, separating adequate performance from inadequate, he desperately needs other sources of information. If the Gentleman relies on proxies and surrogates to carry his messages, by all means, engage these people. They are telling you what the boss is reluctant to say, which is likely to represent the only honest feedback you'll ever receive in the Gentleman's organization.

Avoidance is also a possible strategy, one which I personally employed while working for one of these extreme leaders. Unfortunately, this did not prove to be a very practical tactic. While it did limit the number of awkward, insincere interactions, I was often criticized for not "bringing things to the boss" earlier or more frequently. And although I theoretically could have camped out on his doorstep (I tried this for a while, in fact), I found each interaction with this boss to be horribly uncomfortable. This was largely because behind his soothing words I was always wondering what was really happening.

In this situation, I can only advise the reader NOT to do what I did – it is better to err on the side of over-communication rather than avoidance.

Suck it up. Deal with it. Compared to some of the other extreme leadership types, at least, the Gentleman is relatively easy to stomach.

Part 2

Great Boss

Chapter 12

Qualities that made my Best Boss Great

As I said in the introduction to this book, I've had a lot of bosses over the years. Many of them have been quite successful – both in terms of their own careers as well as in their leadership of high-performing organizations.

But some of these bosses seem to succeed despite themselves. While they might have possessed a handful of over-the-top qualities that drove their success (a towering intellect, an endless supply of drive) or were obsessed with a need to defeat any and all opponents (real or imagined), they were often difficult people. I've often wondered if a top-performing executive can be a "normal" person – normal regarding their relationships and motivations, that is. It sometimes seems that the mega-successful manager reaches her rung on the managerial ladder specifically because of her personality extremes. Based on personal observations, I could easily draw the conclusion that all successful senior managers are just weird – except for the fact that a couple of exceptions blow that theory completely out of the water.

During my years as both a manager and as a subordinate, I've worked for two bosses who were exceptional. Both of them earned my loyalty and respect. And of those two, one, in particular, stands out as my one truly Great Boss. I've often times wondered what it was he did that separated him from the pack. Why was it that I was inspired by him when I've found myself being so critical of the "others"?

Those critical characteristics certainly motivated me to be more committed and more dedicated than at any other time in my career. And while I wouldn't have taken a bullet for my Great Boss, there wasn't much short of such an act for which I wouldn't have volunteered.

I've attempted to sift through my Great Boss' best qualities, teasing out those that made the biggest differences to me. Many of these were characteristics I later tried to emulate during my own climb up the corporate ladder. In this half of the book, I will dissect each of these characteristics, defining the behaviors through examples, describing how my Great Boss demonstrated them, and discussing how they impacted me as a subordinate.

For now, here is the list – the 13 qualities that made my best boss great.

1.   Devoted time to get to know subordinates.
2.   Explained the rationale behind decisions.
3.   Communicated the "big picture."
4.   Gave subordinates a chance to do it their way.
5.   Joined subordinates in the trenches.
6.   Shared key insights.
7.   Helped with career management.

8. Acted boldly.
9. Worked hard.
10. Held his temper.
11. Took the heat.
12. Had credibility up the ladder.
13. Became a friend.

I realize some of these may seem a bit nebulous at this point, a situation that will shortly be resolved as each topic is explored in greater depth. I am aware that many of these characteristics do not appear in a typical "successful management" playbook. A few, in fact, are undoubtedly the opposite of what management gurus would advise. A couple may not be the wisest things to do from a political standpoint.

But all were important elements in making my Great Boss the seasoned, capable executive I came to know. So while adopting these qualities might not necessarily lead you to the CEO's suite, it will definitely help to make you a true and reliable leader in the eyes of your employees.

In my opinion, that is a worthy goal by itself.

Chapter 13

Devoting Time, Building Trust

It doesn't require deep insight to realize most managers suffer from a significant time deficit. Their own bosses make demands, their peers may plot against them, and an ocean of subordinates need direction. As I've said in the past and will undoubtedly say again – the task of management is all about prioritizing and paying attention to the right things.

That's why when a boss devotes the time and energy necessary to get to know you, she is giving you one of the greatest gifts she has to offer. And the technique is even more powerful when the boss lets you get to know her, too. It is also why any subordinate receiving such attention should thank their lucky stars to be so blessed.

A bad example

There were a few of my bosses that I barely seemed to know – I'll call them my "too busy bosses." A "too busy boss" would swoop into my office (or earlier in my career, my desk), rattle off a few rapid-fire sound-bite questions, and then quickly dash off somewhere else, usually before I fully grasped what he wanted.

My relationships with my "too busy bosses" tended to be formal, stuffy, impersonal, and cold. I had little idea what made those bosses tick, and they demonstrated very little commitment to learning what made me tick, as well.

Such bosses are rarely inspirational. Why? Because inspiration and motivation are intensely personal experiences and are hard to achieve at arm's length. We follow people we believe in, that we understand, and that we are convinced have our best interests at heart. If the boss can't make the relationship personal, why follow them?

Developing solid relationships takes time. How strong of a connection can you have when the other person is hard-pressed to remember a single fact about your life (other than the task they've recently assigned to you)?

For most of us, the answer is not strong at all.

Another bad example

Similar to the "too busy boss" was my supervisor who was so guarded that I only encountered her public persona. I'll call this one the "façade boss." I only had one "façade boss," and to her credit, she did spend considerably more time with me than the "too busy bosses." Unfortunately, our time together was rarely productive, as it often felt like I was talking to a robot. Normally, I tried to kill uncomfortable minutes by asking about some obscure business problem or making pointless small-talk – anything to avoid his probing questions and sarcastic observations.

It was obvious to me that "façade boss" was not interested in opening herself up. She was determined that I would never really know the woman behind the mask, and consequently I was hesitant to open myself up, too. This reluctance was reinforced when I later discovered a long list of former subordinates that had nothing positive to say about "façade boss" in the trust department.

Trust is typically earned in the business arena through a process which I call "mutual progressive disclosure." The idea is kind of like the corporate version of what we used to call "Mutually Assured Destruction" during the Cold War. In "mutual progressive disclosure," I know things that can hurt you, and you know things that can hurt me. Trust is established and grown through a slow, step-wise process of bilateral self-revelation. We give a little, and we get a little back. A few (but certainly not all) of the early disclosures can be a little embarrassing or even a bit politically risky, later progressing to a much more complete openness and often an alignment of interests. "Mutual progressive disclosure" doesn't necessarily involve any kind of personal revelation, however. That requires a different kind of disclosure, one that often leads to friendship.

The bottom line is that it's hard to get very far with the "trust thing" if one person in the relationship shows only her veneer.

You can imagine how uninspired I was by both my "too busy boss" and my "façade boss." While I was plenty motivated to work hard on my own, I'm sure I was a pain in the backside in their viewpoints. Without some kind of a relationship that extended beyond formal authority, I felt my own judgment concerning the way things should be done was every bit as valid as that of my boss. And I was plenty headstrong enough to allow myself sometimes to work at cross purposes to anyone I deemed to be a Bad Boss.

A great boss

My best boss invested time in me from the very first day. He hired into the company as a high-ranking VP (later a Group President), and at the time, I was but a lowly manager. We were thrust together in a direct boss-subordinate arrangement without either of us choosing it. As it turned out, none of that mattered. He lavished hours of his precious time on me. He solicited my opinions. He freely offered insights into how things were done in the business world and how corporate leaders thought and behaved. He was sincerely interested in my life outside of work.

In short, we established the give-and-take necessary for mutual trust from his first day on the job. At times, I'm sure he was secretly checking his watch and wondering when I would vacate his office, but he never made me feel unwelcome.

Our best times together were typically lunches, when we could both cast off the immediate burdens of whatever disaster might be unfolding on a particular day and talk about the bigger picture. Sometimes we argued sports. Other times the subject was company strategy or the conduct of those in powerful positions. Occasionally, the focus was a personal problem or challenge I was facing. Regardless of the subject, he was always respectful, interested, and unfailingly made the necessary time for me.

The net effect of these shared experiences was to make me feel like I was, in a complete sense, a full-fledged member of his team. I was a valued person. Almost an equal.

Was I more inspired by this great boss? You bet I was! I would have done almost anything he asked because I learned I could count him as a reliable ally.

The bigger picture

While some of my Great Boss' best characteristics go far beyond just the devotion of time, it all started there. On the first day I met him, we were in the office kitchen pouring coffee, and the pot ran out. As the subordinate, I immediately jumped in to make a fresh pot. He brushed me aside saying that he "…certainly wasn't so important that HE couldn't make the coffee for both of us." In that simple act, he let me know that he considered me to be more than just a lackey. Later that same day, he invited me into his office to talk one-on-one about what I thought he should be accomplishing in his job and how we might succeed in achieving those goals by working together. Yes, *he* invited *me*!

And yes, every hour he devoted to me was an hour he couldn't get back, an hour he couldn't spend working on some other pressing demand. Nevertheless, he recognized the investment would come back to him a hundredfold in the hard work of a dedicated and motivated employee.

Chapter 14

Explaining the Rationale

A step beyond interaction (which I explored in the previous chapter), we have understanding. This chapter delves into how a Great Boss provides rationale a variety of tasks, assignments, jobs, or other projects that may be assign to an employee. In my experience, it is imperative that subordinates understand the larger purpose of the work given to them. This provides them with a connection to the project's overall objectives and prevents them from wasting time on superfluous tasks such as developing elaborate, detailed analyses when a ballpark estimate will do.

Yet such information is all too often withheld from employees for a variety of reasons – secrecy, time deficits, or just a desire to maintain control. In the corporate world, access to information can, indeed, represent power. Instead of a free flow of work rationale from boss to subordinate, generic assignments are often mindlessly doled out by robotic managers while employees labor on, having no idea why.

What not to do

Barking orders is often a boss' path of least resistance. At least, that's the opinion of the "control freak" boss. Orders do keep the plebs on a short leash, parceling out information in tiny chunks on a need-to-know basis. In such an environment, employees have little choice but to follow instructions exactly as they are delivered. Issuing orders might even be the best approach with some employees. I've developed a concept that describes some employees, which I call the "business clueless" – subordinates that make no effort to understand how the business works or show no interest in why they're being told to perform a particular task. Such employees will likely perform most effectively when the "control freak" boss issues a continuous stream of simple instructions. And while there seems to be an abundance of the "business clueless" out there, issuing orders isn't the best way to manage and motivate one's better employees. Not even the average ones for that matter.

At the opposite end of the spectrum from the "control freak" is the "laissez-faire" boss. This type of supervisor obeys a philosophy that looks a lot like plain negligence. The "laissez-faire" boss is either too busy or too uninterested in their employees' work to bother explaining much of anything. This boss simply drops a task in the employee's lap and walks away. It is up to the employee to sort through priorities, possible approaches, potential outcomes, and to navigate the political environment effectively during the process. If the subordinate needs advice, help, or even just a few simple facts, a "laissez-faire" boss is likely nowhere to be found. Employees suffering in this environment are usually forced to rely on peers or others in management to gather the critical information they need to perform their jobs. One thing's for sure – help isn't coming from their overscheduled, under-empathetic boss.

A bad example

While I've seen bosses extensively utilize the command and control approach, issuing detailed directives to employees and expecting those to be followed to the letter, I've never personally worked for one. The closest I came to experiencing a "control freak" boss was by observing a peer who used this approach. When I visited his office, the guy couldn't go more than five minutes without a subordinate timidly tapping on his door to ask for clarification or fresh instruction.

Talking to some of those subordinates, it became clear to me that they were deathly afraid of making a mistake (and yes, punishment did figure highly in this boss' management toolbox). Consequently, they needed constant reassurance that they were doing it the boss' way – particularly when they were worried his way might be the wrong way. For these employees, their boss' approach was stifling, allowing them no opportunity to express their own thinking or creativity – in fact, they were only one step above automatons.

For the boss, the routine he established was also hell – at least, that's the way I interpreted his constant complaining about his subordinates. He became frustrated by the fact that there was little time in his busy day to do anything other than continually issuing more edicts.

Based on what I saw, this type of management style would quickly become self-limiting. This manager could not possibly have handled more than about 6-8 people using his approach, thus making any further progress up the management ladder out of the question.

Another bad example

While I may not have worked for any "control freak" bosses, I did experience plenty subscribing to the "laissez-faire" style. The first of these dated back to the days when I was a mere college student. On the first day in this particular work assignment, my new boss handed me several steel parts and a set of calipers, and then set me in front of a drawing table (yes, a mechanical one, CAD was in its infancy in those days.) He told me to "make a drawing of these parts." After this very brief introduction, he made himself scarce.

I interpreted the assignment as a kind of test, and in the absence of any better information, I set about making blueprint quality drawings. A few days later, new boss expressed surprise at the amount of time it took me to complete the task. As I eventually learned, he would have been completely happy with dimensioned freehand sketches.

Of course, he really didn't care – it was my time that was wasted, which was a commodity he didn't particularly value.

While it is preferable not to bark orders at employees, purposes still need to be clarified, and fully so. I've had some bosses over the years that allowed flexibility in how I accomplished a task but didn't bother explaining its significance to the company. This situation often led to the misapplication of effort, not to mention an employee who felt vaguely betrayed when it sometimes happened that he'd missed the mark.

And one more

In another "laissez-faire" boss scenario, I had a job where I handled technical sales support for an international customer. Despite my best efforts, my boss could not be engaged in discussions about the customer's significance to the company, our objectives with the account, or the strategy being employed to achieve the intended end result (whatever it might have been). In the resulting vacuum, I filled in the blanks myself, making numerous bad assumptions along the way. From my perspective, I was happier with this arrangement than I would have been with a "control freak" boss. That being said, the arrangement certainly led to its fair share of frustration, wasted effort, and more than one major miscue.

In one particular instance, I set to work on the redesign of a competitor's product (the customer having complained to me about the technical performance of this particular item). My plan was to improve the product and thus capture that piece of business from the competition. What I didn't understand at that stage of my career was that there was no money available to make the switch – no matter how much my work improved the product's performance.

As it turned out, I wasted many hours developing a derivative design that ultimately ended up in the hands of our biggest competitor! The customer was quite happy, but other than earning some goodwill, we walked away empty handed.

A little explanation and guidance would have saved me from making a substantial mistake.

A great boss

My best boss' approach to communicating began with an overriding respect for the dignity of his subordinates and flowed from there. Unlike many of my previous bosses, my Great Boss explained the purpose and relevance of my work. We regularly talked through the details of what I was trying to accomplish, the company's overall goals driving the work, possible approaches to solving problems encountered along the way, and the political implications of various potential courses of action.

His clued me in both to the particulars related to specific work assignments and also to the way he thought. Our regular dialog on such subjects was a key element in what made him great.

In contrast to being "laissez-faire," my Great Boss was involved but rarely directive. This was a management style that was undoubtedly challenging to achieve – offering advice, insight, and rationale but still leaving me room to develop my own approach. Most of the time he was able to get this complex equation just right, allowing me to do some of my most effective work while simultaneously permitting me to enjoy my job immensely.

One specific example involved work on an acquisition. My Great Boss and I had several lengthy conversations concerning the advantages and disadvantages of making this purchase. (We called the pluses "Synergies," and minuses "Anergies" – these terms have become titles of two of my corporate thriller novels.) He gave me a free hand regarding the analysis of the deal and in negotiating the contract – freedom which I appreciated. But he was still available when I had questions or became stuck during discussions with the sellers. I learned more from that one project than in a dozen acquisitions I completed later in my career.

The bigger picture

One thing I eventually recognized was different with my Great Boss, different from any boss-subordinate relationship I had before or after – I was able to open up with my Great Boss without any fear of negative consequences. He would talk through issues, concerns, and would even entertain my stupid ideas, without offering direct criticism or consequence. With other bosses, there was often a price to pay when asking for advice or direction – you sometimes looked dumb and experienced a resulting drop in the boss' esteem.

Because of this open and frank communication channel, I was able to learn many of my most valuable management lessons.

I recall one occasion where my Great Boss asked me to help put together one of his presentations. He offered as simple guidance, "…in every presentation I make, I like to provide at least one new insight, conclusion, or piece of information. That's how your superiors know you have something of value to offer." That little observation helped improve every one of my future presentations.

There were dozens of these "ah-ha" moments. My Great Boss effectively passed along a career's worth of hard-won knowledge through our daily interactions. And without expending a huge amount of effort, he aided my career far more than any other boss.

In the instances when I've successfully employed the same strategy as a boss, I've also experienced my share of "ah-ha's." These have mostly occurred when a subordinate developed a novel or better way of doing something than what I had envisioned. In those instances, I try to remember to thank my lucky stars that I provided gentle guidance rather than issuing orders or ignoring my subordinate completely.

Remember, when your boss is willing to explain but not direct, he is offering you a gift – the gift of his years of experience, broader perspective, and keen insight. Such assistance is a palpable demonstration of her respect for your value as an employee and demonstrates that she places importance on your education, development, and contribution.

A boss that fails to explain the rationale behind your work cannot truly be called "great."

Chapter 15

Communicating the Big Picture

Alignment.

It's a term we hear over and over when discussing the responsibilities of those in charge. A leader's job (among other things) is to get everyone on the same page.

Alignment means making one's personal goals and aspirations consistent with something, and in a typical business environment that "something" is invariably the firm's spoken and unspoken strategies, tactics, objectives, competitive reality, and the overall organization's culture. Rolled together, these various subjects of alignment can be summarized by the term the "big picture."

It is certainly possible to lead a team of subordinates without them understanding the first thing about the big picture or where they fit into it, but doing so would require extreme oversight. The idea of directing a team without giving them the big picture reminds me of an odd test I was given years ago when I was interviewing. In this test, I was given a pile of wood and various bits of hardware (mostly nuts and bolts) along with a set of plans and told to construct the structure pictured. I wasn't, however, permitted to touch any of the parts. Instead, I was given two "workers" who were my hands. And unlike a typical team member, my "workers" only followed my literal instructions. They would simply wander off if I failed to give them a job to complete. The entire exercise was timed and graded.

Needless to say, the test was completely exhausting and more than a bit frustrating at times. My takeaway was that without a broader understanding of what we were trying to accomplish, managing my "workers" – only two of them – quickly became almost impossible. To get them to help me intelligently and effectively accomplish the goal (building the structure) required that, among other things, they understand the "big picture" of the project as well as I. Without that understanding, alignment was impossible, which was the point of the entire exercise.

In a broad sense, it makes sense to explore in greater detail what's included in the "big picture." Strategy and tactics are definitely a part of what an employee needs to know. Most employees can learn the formal part of these on their own simply by paying attention to presentations and reading printed materials. Interpretation and distillation, the translation of airy, high-level strategies to the working level in the company, is where the rubber meets the road for a manager. This is also where the "big picture" becomes meaningful to the individual. When the boss doesn't provide interpretation, it is often done by peers, subordinates, or even a collection of corporate malcontents. If you're lucky enough to have a Great Boss, she becomes your first and best source for interpretation of the company's strategy.

The "big picture" doesn't stop there. It also includes what are sometimes unspoken goals and aspirations, ones that may be indirectly driving the organization. It includes an understanding of competitors and their SWOTs (strengths, weaknesses, opportunities, and threats). This is an area I've found most companies seem to capture poorly, preferring simply to mischaracterize their opponents as either "evil" or "stupid."

And then there's this amorphous blob known as "culture," a difficult constituent to define and one that is clearly also a part of the "big picture." Culture might best be thought of as the history, personality, traditions, reputation, and folklore of the organization which is shaped by its past. What does the organization believe motivates employees? Greed? A greater mission? Something else? That's definitely a part of the culture. One can also toss in the informal power system of the organization, a set of unwritten rules and relationships that define how things "get done." Also a part of the culture.

The Great Boss will make all these elements of the "big picture," many of which are shrouded in mystery, much clearer for the average employee.

And when that happens, it normally results in greatly improved alignment. Not perfect, but better. It would be nice if such alignment were seamless, but that never happens. Subordinates still have their personal ambitions, goals, and beliefs, some of which always exhibit a degree of conflict with the objectives of the organization.

What not to do

Over the years, I've come across four ineffective approaches bosses use to communicate the "big picture" to their subordinates. I've labeled these approaches as benign neglect, command and control, bits and pieces, and the blind leading the blind. Each one, while different, essentially leave subordinates in the same place – with a poor or even non-existent understanding of the "big picture" and how they fit within it.

Benign neglect

Certainly the most common of the failed approaches, with benign neglect the boss communicates none of the "big picture" to their subordinates, generally considering it unimportant. This is the business equivalent of casting a new swimmer out into deep water and letting them fend for themselves. For the boss, it is an effortless approach to handling subordinates, its greatest advantage being that it saves time and energy for other priorities. When talking to some bosses about their benign neglect approach, I've heard a couple rationalize the behavior as a form of social Darwinism. The idea seems to be that those employees destined to survive will eventually catch on to what they need to know. The rest ultimately move onto other jobs (usually at other companies).

For the employee, benign neglect results in confusion, wasted effort, frustration, and sometimes anger that only occasionally seems to be directed where it belongs – at their supervisor.

One of my bosses practiced this approach, and sometimes I had the impression she got her jollies watching me (and others) miscue. I remember one instance where I was nominated for a company scholarship award, and she offered me nothing in terms of advice on how to handle the selection interviews. I ended up making a really stupid statement to one of my interviewers because I was unaware of a personal issue with which he was struggling. Of course, when I discovered my gaff, I was mortified. When I relayed the story to my boss, she just shrugged her shoulders, clearly uninterested. Could he have helped me navigate my way through that discussion? Without a doubt.

I was happy to move to another boss a short time later.

Command and control

The classic management approach to alignment is simply to order people to do what you want and not worry about their grasp of the "why." This approach is simple, but the effectiveness – as I illustrated in my "structure building" exercise at the beginning of this chapter – is generally quite poor. Command and control approaches generally require immense amounts of effort over time to maintain.

Employees find this style to be stifling. People work better and more diligently when they know why their efforts are needed, not when they're simply given commands. The bottom line is the "why" matters, and if the boss doesn't provide it, he'll likely end up with lots of wasted time and a group of unhappy subordinates.

One of my earliest bosses was of the command and control persuasion. He always had a ready set of orders for me, most of which consisted of the classic "do this, not that" type of direction. I was part of a painting team and recall one day when he ordered our entire work team to "scrape off every speck of old paint" from a set of tall columns. He apparently didn't notice the detailed scrollwork at the top we devoted hours to scrape paint meticulously off of the underlying plaster (while making a mess of parts of it, as you can imagine). Had he taken the time to explain that we only needed to address the "loose stuff" up at the top because it was so far from the ground, we would have saved hours and hours. But that wasn't his style.

The team labeled the boss "a jerk," and he undoubtedly thought of all of us as "idiots." Perhaps that was fair. We were all young and untested. I think the term "inexperienced," however, would have been more accurate.

The point is that the entire episode could have been avoided if he'd just taken the time to explain the big picture.

Bits and pieces

Another one of my bosses enjoyed doling out pieces of the big picture a few at a time. I was much further along in my career when I encountered this manager and was much less likely to allow her game playing to force me into an error. Still, I found her style to be quite annoying.

At one particular board dinner, she paired me with the most difficult director of the company and offered no words of counsel or insight. I was new to the organization at the time, and I dutifully asked for advice concerning how I should handle the inevitable conversation. Her response was to give me a thirty-second, fifty-thousand-foot overview of the difficult director and then suggested I "let him (the board member) do all the talking."

As it turned out, that was a good idea, but hardly practical when the director has you cornered during a two-hour meal. My boss had given me about ten percent of what I needed to handle the situation well, which meant I inadvertently misstepped a time or two – fortunately not seriously. The only thing that prevented me from experiencing a disaster was the advice I'd picked up from peers and the few other things I figured out on the fly.

In the end, the meal could have been characterized as a modest success, but no thanks to my boss who was devoted to doling out his insights one sliver at a time.

Blind leading the blind

Another boss, affable enough, was the perfect example of the blind leading the blind. No matter how good your intentions, you can't lead people to a better understanding of the big picture when you don't have that understanding yourself. This boss thought she had keen insight when it came to meeting the needs of her superior, and she had no hesitation in offering this valuable information to any and all of her subordinates.

Except most of the time, she was wrong. On par, though I enjoyed working for this woman (she had a lot of other good qualities), she was virtually useless when it came to growing my understanding of the company.

Some managers simply aren't constructed in a way that allows them to grasp how it all fits together, despite their best intentions. This boss was one of them.

A great boss

I remember the first time my Great Boss gave me a glimpse of the big picture. We were sitting down to lunch, and he observed that "…at Company X (our employer) it's pretty clear you get yelled at for missing sales targets, but you'll be fired for missing on profits."

It was an observation that would have taken me years to come up with on my own. I was impressed that he saw it after only a few weeks on the job, (I had been with the company longer than he.) I was even more impressed that he was willing to pass it along.

Over the three years we worked together, we spent quite a bit of time talking about multiple aspects of the company's "big picture." These discussions covered subjects ranging from internal politics to industry strategy to the individual personalities of important executives. During these discussions, I learned many things. We discussed how our business strategy was designed to foil a key strength of a particularly difficult-to-dislodge competitor. I recall talks about the behaviors absolutely required to succeed personally at the company. And we chatted about some potential pitfalls that could undermine a manager's career – both with our particular employer and in the corporate world at large.

The bigger picture

What made this boss great was not only that he could see all of this clearly, but more importantly that he was willing to share it with his subordinates. Some of his abilities came to him more easily because of his greater experience, while in other areas he was simply more perceptive. While I would benefit less today from these insights and observations (being able to discover the truth for myself more readily now that I, too, am more experienced,) I would still value his willingness to share critical information.

Chapter 16

Providing a Chance to Fail

This notion – that employees need an opportunity to fail – is undoubtedly counter-intuitive to many managers. In most people's minds, failing is catastrophic. Failure is a disaster to be avoided at all costs. And under most circumstances, I couldn't agree more – failure is, at least, a label that must be avoided like the plague.

Unless you work for a Great Boss.

Over time, I have come to realize that allowing me a chance to fail was one of the key things that made my best boss great. I'm not describing the common practice of casting someone out into the deep water without a life ring and hoping they'll learn to swim. Structured chances to fail were carefully orchestrated by my boss and were designed to stretch and test me. They generally excluded the potential for a career-ending meltdown. As a result of meeting and (mostly) succeeding with these challenges, I advanced my management skills and insights much more rapidly under my Great Boss' tutelage than under any other supervisor.

And it was actually enjoyable.

What not to do

I've experienced managers on both ends of the spectrum – either they send you out to slay dragons while underequipped and overmatched or they micromanage you every step along the way. Identifying an employee that is ready to grow and develop can be tough, and getting the touch with that employee just right is even tougher. But it can be done, no matter where the subordinate is along their personal developmental path – neophyte to journeyman and everywhere between.

Hands off

It would be a mistake to identify the "hands off" approach utilized by many managers as equivalent to simple "benign neglect" that I discussed in the previous chapter. In truth, there is an element of devious politicking involved in pushing unready employees into deep water. "Hands-off" managers tend to leave subordinates to their own devices, knowing full well that if things go wrong, the subordinate could easily be blamed. If the disaster becomes too large, such an employee could be readily discarded. Elsewhere, I've identified such behavior as "scapegoating," a most pernicious political tactic.

Some managers, in fact, are so adept at using this technique that they line up a scapegoat for every challenging assignment or edgy project. Even the most generous excuse for this behavior – that the manager is "too busy" to be involved to the degree necessary to evaluate properly and guide the subordinate relative to the task at hand – represents bad management in the extreme.

One of my bosses fell squarely into this category. When things went wrong, he invariably pushed a scapegoat into the breach, often one that was eventually fired for not turning the proverbial "sow's ear" into the desired "silk purse." He described this process as "going up" when there was a problem as opposed to "diving down" into the details in an attempt to render assistance. Eventually, it became my turn to be the hapless, sacrificial victim of this Machiavellian management method. I freely admit, however, that I helped nominate myself for corporate martyrdom by making a series of high-risk calls at what turned out to be the exact wrong time.

Most of the lessons I learned from this bad example of subordinate management involved how to politic effectively and blame others – hardly the stuff that helps a person develop into a Great Boss.

Hands on

At the other extreme is the Micromanager, who is often seen by his superiors as being "hands on." These bosses, for whatever reason, seem to find it impossible to give subordinates enough leeway to make even the pettiest of decisions or to attempt to implement anything of their own devising. I suspect this "style" of management has its roots in either a feeling of insecurity (a manager unsure if he will make it in his job) or inadequacy (a manager that subconsciously isn't confident that he deserves the success he's already experienced). I've also witnessed a few bosses who appear to be overly confident that their way is always the right way, if not the only way. Regardless of the motivation driving "hands-on" behavior, the effect is pretty much the same – oppressive, suffocating oversight and endless second-guessing.

I had one boss that nominally fell into this category, although he was far from the worst "hands-on" manager I've ever seen. Because I was pretty far along in my career at that time, I found his constant need to drive every aspect of every decision to be beyond annoying. I eventually left that position, and, at least, part of my motivation for the move was the consistent feeling that "the town wasn't big enough for the both of us."

A great boss

Perhaps I was at the perfect point in my career (no longer wet behind the ears but still before the midpoint) when I encountered my Great Boss. He certainly seemed to have an instinct about when to give me a chance to show my stuff and just how far to let me go without a check-in or a check-up. I saw him manage his more senior people with a slightly different technique, giving them more freedom to act but still not just turning them loose when they might venture into unfamiliar territory. I suspect that a newbie employee would have found him providing substantially more (but still wholly appropriate) guidance.

Part of what made this work was a sense that I can only call "touch." He seemed to recognize the degree of involvement each of his subordinates needed and was able to tune his technique to provide just that much and no more. When we reviewed progress on my projects, for example, his method was Socratic – he asked me leading questions that ultimately brought me to conclusions that were better than I would have arrived at on my own. The keys to this were the "ah-ha's" that were mine to experience, exactly what I needed from a developmental standpoint at that moment. And I was free to argue and even reject his advice, which I did on occasion.

One project I headed – a small, bolt-on acquisition – taught me much of what I know about doing deals. This is knowledge I put to use repeatedly in subsequent years. There were many meetings with my boss to discuss elements of the valuation, the direction of the negotiation, how to present the opportunity for the CEO's approval, and even what the post-acquisition integration plan should look like. He corrected my course on numerous occasions, but he never told me "do it like this." Figuring out how to pull off the deal successfully was my responsibility alone. And he never, ever used any foolish statement or demonstrated weaknesses from the process against me in appraisals or in determining my next job assignment – at least if he did so, I remained blissfully unaware.

The acquisition ultimately went through and was integrated into the business unit with minimal issues. I owed much of the success of the project to my boss' guidance, but I could still claim the victory as my own.

The bigger picture

The objective of providing me chances to fail was to make sure I owned my decisions but to do so in a manner that each outcome also provided a teaching opportunity. My Great Boss wanted me fully aware of the implications of the direction I was proposing and the actions I was contemplating, and ultimately to take full responsibility for each project.

I loved the environment he created.

In the later years of my career, I attempted to emulate his technique with my subordinates. While I know I often failed to stay true to this lesson (I have a tendency to be a bit too "hands on" at times), I thought that by and large I succeeded with most of my direct reports. I hope this was to their long-term benefit. As a side benefit to me, I've had numerous epiphanies when the solution proposed by my subordinate turned out to be significantly better than anything I would have dreamed up on my own. Providing chances to fail increased my team's capacity to the point where it encompassed the sum total of all our skills, rather than being limited by me.

Subordinates develop more quickly with skin in the game, but there is no substitute for the knowledge of an experienced hand – the trick is bringing both to a project at the same time. Getting the formula for this correct can be difficult, but when you are successful, you unlock the hidden potential in your subordinates. Give your people guidance, but also provide them with a chance to fail based on their own merits and abilities. And preferably provide it in situations where failure doesn't spell severe damage to their careers.

Chapter 17

Sharing the Trenches

One of my less-than-stellar bosses was once described by a peer as "…standing on the shore, throwing rocks" anytime one of her subordinates headed into rough water. I can attest to the fact that this boss rarely lifted a finger to help her subordinates and absolutely never put herself in the way of potential trouble. As a result, my peers and I were denied an opportunity to see the boss in action. We were also denied the opportunity to learn from her reasoning and her experience. And most importantly, we were denied the chance to really reach for big successes because we all knew that, in the end, the outcome would rest entirely on our shoulders.

My Great Boss approached similar situations from the opposite perspective. He was in the boat with me and usually paddling like hell – just like I was. When a tough situation arose, we worked together to sort out problems. When a proposal was put forward, he advocated as strongly as I did. We were a team, and I never worried that he might abandon me.

What not to do

Standing aloof and allowing subordinates to sink or swim on their own may sometimes seem like a good approach to managing. It does, after all, protect the boss by offering him a ready scapegoat to sacrifice should a major catastrophe arise. This is particularly true when the company is one of those committed to the search for the guilty (and the associated punishment of the innocent). Such an approach may work by offering the manager a modicum of protection, but it's hardly inspirational and it denies subordinates the opportunity to utilize the best the manager has to offer – his strategic insight, his reasoning, his experience, and most importantly his commitment.

When a manager takes this position, subordinates quickly realize that they are alone – with predictable results. Employees will take few, if any, risks and will search for their own scapegoats to blame when things go wrong. Under such circumstances, many subordinates won't hesitate to toss the boss under the bus should the opportunity arise. It's a cutthroat world out there, but one many of us face nearly every day as a part of corporate America. At least, this is the rationale frequently offered when a manager allows a subordinate to take the fall for them.

Alas, this is the way things often flow.

An example

The boss I mentioned in this chapter's first paragraph was probably the most egregious abuser of abandoning subordinates I've ever encountered. I recall one incident where a subordinate (one of my peers) went around the boss making contacts higher on the corporate ladder. I eventually learned this peer had tried to build a case for why she should be promoted and why our mutual boss should be fired! Of course, this backfired, and it was only a few months before the boss found a pretense to terminate the ambitious subversive. Although the firing was explained away as "a restructuring," no one was fooled. By going behind the boss' back – his only alternative, in his opinion – the subordinate had nominated himself to be a victim. The underlying problem, however, was that the subordinate had desperately wanted the boss to help him position himself to be an eventual successor, but the aloof boss would have none of it. It had only been a matter of time before the boss eliminated a valued employee that had morphed into an erstwhile competitor.

This kind of thing would have never happened with my Great Boss. In the first place, his subordinates would have never found themselves politicking behind his back. Why would they? He was our best advocate when it came to career advancement. When I expressed an interest in moving my career forward, he became my backer, helping to find the right job and aiding me in convincing the CEO that I was the right pick for it.

Besides, our collaborative relationship would have made going around his back completely unthinkable. In a sense, my Great Boss' best defense against being undermined by his own people was his strong offense – nobody would try to injure him when he was laboring hard on their behalf.

Another example

In another incident, I recall this same Bad Boss denying ownership of a particularly unfavorable distribution contract, one that I knew for a fact she'd personally negotiated and signed. When the contract became an issue several years after it had been inked, there was no way she was going to own up to her role in it. Unfortunately, this left me stuck with a messy relationship and little insight into how it had gotten that way. I suspect she desperately wanted to avoid blame for the contract's defects – dodging responsibility seemed to be an objective uppermost on her mind.

I sure could have used her insight into the context of that agreement and a better understanding of why it was written as it was. Even more, I had hoped she would get directly involved, joining me in the renegotiation and working what was clearly a complex relationship with the distributor. Without any assistance, renegotiating became an elaborate game of pin the tail on the donkey, with me guessing what the leverage points in the contract might be and making plenty of mistakes. After my initial approach, it became clear that the contract was seen as a personal risk by my Bad Boss, and there was no possible way she would be stepping into the trenches with me, not for any conceivable reason. In fact, if there were a blow up during the negotiations, I knew she would have merrily fed me to her superiors as "the cause" of the problem.

See what I mean by "standing on the shore, tossing rocks?"

In the end, I was forced to make numerous concessions to the distributor – ones that might not have been necessary if the boss had owned up to her involvement in the original contract and then stepped in to help clean up her own mess. The outcome was undoubtedly far worse for the company than it needed to be.

A great boss

Every major project or critical program was a shared effort with my best boss. While I might have done most of the heavy lifting, I never had the impression that he was anything other than a full and committed partner in the effort.

This benefited me in several ways, the greatest of which was that when I encountered heavy sledding I could count on him to back me up no matter what. Many of my other bosses would have hesitated to lend their support when the pressure was on, afraid that they might get "dirt" on them when a reluctant CEO's opinion couldn't easily be turned. Not my Great Boss – I could count on him to be by my side if I started to bow under the pressure of intense cross-examination. In fact, I went into high-risk encounters knowing he would protect me if things really went south.

And now, a positive example

While I worked for my greatest boss, we developed a new corporate strategy, one designed to neutralize one of the key strengths relied upon by our number one competitor. The presentation of this strategy was technical and complex, requiring a high degree of patience to understand fully. Unfortunately, the intended audience, our CEO, was anything but patient. Within a few slides, he was on his feet challenging most of our assumptions and all of our conclusions.

Most bosses would have waited passively on the sidelines, silently watching as I was verbally flayed (We all know it is much easier to criticize than construct.) Not my Great Boss. He stepped directly into the fray. First, he tried to take some of the questions with which I was struggling. When that didn't stop the onslaught, he got testy with the

CEO (a Screamer), something I would have never done. After a few tense minutes, the presentation was back on track. In the end, the CEO grudgingly accepted our strategy (subject to a few minor modifications he insisted upon – window dressing, in my humble opinion). Subsequently, its implementation drove growth in the business for more than a decade.

Chapter 18

Providing Key Insights

Most of us consider ourselves to be reasonably discerning. After all, we depend on our perceptiveness to protect us from danger, to give us guidance into how to manage our behavior, and to let us know when there are opportunities to exploit. Here's a tip – you're probably not as good at it as you think. Many people seem to misperceive the motives behind the actions of others – and when they err, they tend to err on the side of assuming others are more like they are than is actually the case.

Perceptiveness is one of those qualities that is a small part inborn talent (you come into the world with a certain capacity for it) and a bigger part learned (you can improve your game with patience, effort, and experience). As it turns out, I was granted less of the natural talent portion of this critical skill than many of my business peers. As a result, I urgently needed to develop my abilities in this area.

The question was: How?

There is no course on "perceptiveness" in the MBA program at Harvard, and no formal training on it at GM or Emerson Electric (or probably anywhere else, for that matter). It is, like many managerial skills, largely an experiential capability – one developed primarily through practice and use.

By the time I started working for my best boss, it was clear that solely relying on my own experiences to improve my perceptiveness was probably not going to get me to where I wanted to go. Not that I hadn't made some progress, but I was still stepping on a lot of toes while learning lessons by making mistakes. Some of this was funny and forgivable, like when I would automatically (and often incorrectly) assign boss/subordinate roles when meeting people for the first time. Other times it was horribly embarrassing, like the time I loudly asked a superior about his new baby only to discover that the child had recently passed away.

It was clear I wasn't reading people well enough to prevent occasional catastrophic errors – something which I needed to be able to correct if I were to function as an effective leader.

Fortunately, it was at this point in time that I went to work for my best boss. He became my sensei in the art and science of perceptiveness. I became his student, gobbling up every insight and every bit of advice he had to offer on the subject. To my great benefit, not only was he completely free with his observations into the corporate world, but he was also very skilled in this area.

What not to do
Perceptiveness skills vary all over the map within management ranks, ranging from excellent to stunningly

bad. For your manager to have a hope of helping you, he needs to be better at it than you are.

Your boss could be quite skillful in this area, however, and still not offer you any aid. Not all bosses are willing to share insights with their subordinates. And some are willing to share the conclusions, but not the process they use to arrive at them. In fact, I've found the willingness to share to be a relatively rare predisposition on the part of bosses. I suspect the reason for this is that there can be a relatively high degree of political risk involved. After all, a subordinate might be loyal to someone else in the organization – a possible enemy. Or perhaps, the subordinate is a hopeless gossip, and anything sensitive the boss passes along will quickly become the subject of public ogling. And then there is the occasional subordinate that thinks they can take down their boss. Sharing insights with such a character is just inviting him to try to take your job.

Or a bad boss might simply be satisfied with the status quo and indifferent to helping his people. Beyond skills and a willingness to share, the boss has to have an interest in helping you improve your perceptiveness skills. The improbable coexistence of high skill, manageable perceived risk, and a willingness to help already tells you that getting this kind of assistance from your boss is going to be quite rare.

Throughout my years in large corporations, I had only one boss (other than my Great Boss) that attempted to "take me under his wing." He attempted to provide me with insights about how the formal and informal power chain worked within the company. Unfortunately, he was only slightly more capable in this area than I, a textbook example of the phrase "…the blind leading the blind."

Most managers simply don't offer to share key insights. If asked, they might give you a taste, but they will often hold back when it comes to particularly sensitive observations – fearing their revelation may somehow hurt them. Even if you are offered an illustration of how they are able to recognize certain truths and trends, you need to temper that victory with the understanding that you might not be learning it from a particularly insightful source.

An example

One of my bosses was particularly insightful into the company's political process, but he guarded that information closely. At the time, I was a fledgling first-line production supervisor and had recently terminated an employee for sleeping while on the job. My boss told me to expect the employee back (without offering any understanding into how he knew this) and sure enough, a few days later my snoozing subordinate was back on the job. My boss clearly had keen insight into what would happen during the grievance process, but he wasn't willing to share.

Over time, I ran across a few bosses that were similarly tight-lipped, but more common were those bosses that seemed to be more clueless than I.

Another example

In one particular instance, I had a boss that publicly pilloried one of my peers for refusing a trip to Europe (he'd just been over there the prior week, and the need was debatable). Not surprisingly my peer soon quit, but my boss seemed to have been taken completely unaware when his boss and corporate HR extensively interrogated him over the exchange. And while there was no obvious, immediate consequence for my boss' poor judgment, I suspect incidents of this type coalesced the thoughts of those higher in management into a pretty good image of that man's insightfulness, or lack thereof.

Clearly, there wasn't a lot to be learned from this manager.

My great boss

With my best boss, the dynamic was completely different from what I had experienced with almost every previous supervisor. He not only regularly offered his insights to me, he was also ready to explain how he'd gained them, including detailing his sources, explaining how he interpreted subtle words and actions and confirming whom he might approach when needing to verify uncertain conclusions.

For my part, I was a sponge, soaking up everything he said on the subject of perceptiveness and often asking my own probing questions. Eventually, I brought my own uncertainties to the table and asked for his interpretations. Under those circumstances, he rarely gave me a direct answer, but instead insisted on leading me there by asking a series of questions. One such discussion involved my next job. That conversation went something like this…

Great Boss: Where do you see yourself in five years?

Me: I don't know, maybe as a division president (said tentatively while flinching a bit).

GB: That might be too long for you to wait for that to happen. Let's say for now that I agree with your goal to earn a job in general management, but we might want to speed things up a bit. Ideally, how would you get there?

Me: I suppose I'd move into management at one of the smaller divisions in a job reporting to the division president – preferably one where I came in as the acknowledged *Heir Apparent* (the title of one of my novels).

GB: And then you'd what? Just wait for something to happen?

Me: I suppose I could try to pick a division where the president is likely to retire soon. Or one where he is likely to be promoted.

GB: Good thinking. What functional role would you want to take on?

Me: I don't know. I'm probably strongest in operations.

GB: What part of your background needs the most strengthening?

Me: Probably sales and marketing.

The conversation continued along this vein until it became clear to me exactly what the ideal assignment looked like. We talked about the corporate perception of my next promotion, the overall timing (what would be too quick – less than a year – and what would be too long – more than three years). We even discussed how to make a noticeable impact on my next job in the short term and what I could do that might improve my chances of ultimately succeeding to the job.

Notice he asked me leading questions. Most of the discussion were him listening to what I wanted and getting me to think about the best path to reach my goal. Maybe there was a little subtle manipulation, but I certainly didn't see it that way at the time. If there was, it was most certainly benevolent.

Ultimately, I ended up taking a job as VP of Sales, Marketing, and Strategic Planning at a small division, one that reported directly to my Great Boss. The current division President was sixty-two years old and was likely to retire in the next few years. Nothing was guaranteed, but by working with my boss, I knew I was positively positioning myself for the most important promotion of my life – my first job as a general manager.

The bigger picture

Most bosses aren't interested in offering you the benefit of their insights, much less instructing you on how they gained it in the first place. My best boss did all of that and more. Doing so took a willingness to take a chance on a person he didn't know well, recognizing that by putting himself at moderate risk he would either earn my undying loyalty or quickly discover I wasn't worth the effort. That's what real leaders do – they go beyond the mechanical elements of day-to-day management to inspire and motivate those that work around them. On this dimension alone, my best boss qualified as a great leader.

Chapter 19

Aiding with Career Management

Many supervisors claim they help their subordinates manage and develop their careers. In most cases, this means that they examine educational background and experience, looking for any "unchecked boxes," and offer impractical, semi-generic advice about how those unchecked boxes are limiting the person. Such advice is, in my personal experience, useless at best and at times can be downright damaging.

A better boss helps you identify what behaviors or characteristics are holding you back (I'll talk about this in detail a little later in this chapter when I discuss "elevator reviews") and offers practical ideas you can apply. Beyond that, she provides frank recommendations on next steps and identifies when you are wasting your time. A better boss will provide you observations you are unlikely to make on your own and might also add insights into how things work at the company.

My Great Boss went beyond this – having open discussions with me about where I wanted to go and how to position myself to get there. And THEN HE MADE IT HAPPEN. My best boss was completely open and honest with me about where I stood in the pecking order. He helped identify my deficits. And he was willing to take personal risks on my behalf to change the trajectory of my career.

What not to do – bad bosses
"You need to finish your degree."
"You need experience in product management."
"You need an MBA."
"You need experience working in Division X."

This is the kind of "shoot from the hip" career advice you'll get from a less-than-stellar boss. It is typically offered with little contemplation of your specific circumstances, skills, and capabilities and mainly covers what might be seen as "holes" in your resume. Never mind the fact that getting an MBA or working in product management will often provide absolutely zero practical assistance in getting you to your next promotion.

The superficial advice of this type is all about removing paper objections, things that a theoretical hiring manager might use to screen out an "undesirable" candidate. The theory seems to go that if you eliminate all objections, the hypothesized hiring manager will no longer have the ability to turn you down for the job. It seems silly when you think about it, but I've seen more than one employee waste enormous amounts of time and effort trying to check these boxes. They are more than frustrated when they discover there are other, steeper barriers to overcome.

Finishing a degree, moving to a distant location, or changing functional areas are not trivial undertakings. They disrupt lives, introduce additional career risks, and can sometimes cost a pretty penny. An employee shouldn't be advised to take these steps unless a tangible improvement in their career is nearly a sure thing.

These wasted efforts occur largely because most employees are clueless when it comes to their own performance (or lack, thereof). I offer as evidence a study I saw years ago which showed that roughly 80% of employees believe they are in the top 10% of company performers. Clearly, there's plenty of self-delusion to go around. And if they don't know their own performance, they understand senior management's perceptions of it even less. Part of the employee's problem is simply wishful thinking, which makes them susceptible to this "paint by numbers" approach to creating their own "career masterpiece."

On the boss' side, stopping at this level of career advice is most likely a combination of laziness, limited perception, and a desire to avoid any kind of difficult conversation. I've seen all three factors in play in varying proportions during my career.

Possibly the most common action taken under this kind of "advice" is pursuing educational objectives (most often an MBA or completing an undergraduate degree). In most cases, when the boss offers this as her advice, I think it is simply a way of "kicking the can down the road" and thus avoiding an uncomfortable confrontation. Following such advice, employees make substantial personal (and often financial) sacrifices. They are subsequently shocked when they discover – degree in hand – that management at the company views them exactly the same way they had done before they were awarded their sheepskin.

Not to say that an MBA is useless. I personally decided to go to school full time to earn my MBA – at least in part because I was finding myself stuck in technical roles when my interests were running in the direction of impacting the direction of the overall business. Interestingly, I came to the decision to pursue an MBA on my own, rather than having it "presented" to me by a lazy boss.

An example

I had a low-level manager working in my organization while in one of my general management positions. Under the previous regime, this manager had been counseled that promotional doors were closed to her because she didn't have an MBA. Being an ambitious employee, she took courses at night at the local community college and eventually collected her degree after many years of hard work, some strained relationships at home, and a depleted savings account.

Then she came to see me, stating that she was "ready" for a promotion. She wanted to know what I had available – as if jobs in the company were sitting on shelves just waiting for the right applicant to come along and ask for them. I had the unpleasant experience of having to bring her expectations back down to earth. The problem was, this particular employee was... odd. She had few social skills and basically no emotional intelligence. Her few subordinates hated working for her. She had other excellent qualities, but her defects were what limited her, not the lack of a degree. I was quite certain my predecessor sent her off to get the credential simply to temporarily stop her from asking for promotions.

It was pure laziness. A laziness that cost the employee years of hard work and thousands of dollars, not to mention all kinds of regrets when it came to her family.

The story had a happy ending, however. The employee, realizing that I was never going to promote her, eventually quit. Last I heard, she was a consultant – a job that was much better suited to her skills and minimized her shortcomings. The career change worked out well and today she appears to be quite happy. Things don't always turn out so nicely.

Good bosses

As in my previous example, most people have something they do (or don't do) that holds back the progress of their career. I did. You probably do, too. Maybe there are several things. The problem is, if you take superficial career advice from a Bad Boss, you'll likely never figure out what you really need to work on to get ahead.

As human beings, we seem extraordinarily adept at self-deception. We can quickly find the "fatal flaw" in a peer – the thing that is preventing her from being promoted – but we rarely see our own. In fact, even when someone hints around at our biggest weaknesses, most of us find ways to rationalize away any critical feedback. It seems that only through direct confrontation or disaster (such as being fired) do we really get a glimpse at our biggest deficiencies.

This thought is what inspired a change in the way I wrote performance reviews for my people, converting a couple of pages of checkboxes into what I called the "elevator review." An elevator review is easier for the boss to prepare and much more impactful than the typical, hated, check-box, annual review.

Here's how it works:

I make a list of two or possibly three strengths the employee commands and balance that against one or two of their biggest failings. All of the items I identify are the kind of thing I would mention to my boss if she asked about the employee and I had only 2-3 minutes to respond.

In my experience, managers are often called upon to summarize an employee in just this fashion to their superiors, and it is best to be prepared. But I don't keep this to myself or offer it only to my boss. The employee and I have a frank conversation about "the good, the bad, and the ugly" and how her future can be changed/improved.

The "elevator review" came about as a result of two things. First was the realization that the traditional review forms never correctly portray the picture of the employee. It is far too easy to mark lots of things as "above average" and then soft-pedal the one or two big problem areas. Employees are usually left with the impression that their "pros" massively outweighed their "cons," and in many cases they conclude they are one of their boss' best performers.

Yes, we have a deluded workforce!

The second reason was my own frequent reflection on the most meaningful review I ever received. It was one I had been given years earlier – a traditional form review, but one that ended with a poignant summary. I recall exactly what my boss wrote in that final box: "Gets a lot done, but sometimes pisses people off." It was my first "elevator review," and it had more impact on me than a career's worth of checkbox forms.

Taking it up to "11" – a great boss

My best boss went beyond simply conducting "elevator review" types of discussions with me – which we had numerous times, not just as an annual event. He actually took positive actions on my behalf to move my career along. Working together, we identified my long-term target position. He even created an interim job that would help me gain the necessary experience and credibility in a functional area with which I was unfamiliar (sales). He also sold his boss on the job move and made sure I was taken care of financially. When the target job opened up, he again advocated for me, helping me to win the position despite being the youngest employee in company history ever to move into a Divisional President job.

While I know he didn't go this far for all his employees, everyone that directly reported to him (and was a loyal, committed, solid contributor) got at least a portion of my best boss' valuable career management package.

The bigger picture

It is one thing to offer low-risk, off-the-cuff advice about career management to a subordinate. It is quite another to take the time and potential political risk to dig deep in order to help the employee make their dreams a reality. Weak supervisors rarely go to the effort of actually assisting their employees. Better bosses will be more insightful, but will often stop short of putting themselves at risk by aggressively advocating for a subordinate. The best managers, however, will do almost anything to help a valued direct report advance and grow – that's one of the key things that make them great bosses.

Chapter 20

Taking Bold Actions

Some people are visionaries, able to paint a clear and compelling picture of the future and outline the strategy to get there. Others are excellent tacticians by nature, able to take the visionary's work and turn it into an executable plan. Still others are followers, making their best contribution in the implementation of the plans put in place by others. Companies need people of every variety. Not all of them can be visionaries or tacticians – although there is a greater proportion of such employees in the managerial ranks, where their particular talents for strategy and tactics are best utilized.

Along another dimension, most companies want their employees to be biased toward taking small risks (or none at all), but there is also a need for the big risk takers. Those people willing to "bet the farm," when right, rapidly propel a company forward into the future.

My Great Boss combined a visionary, strategic capability with a willingness to take large but measured risks through a set of behaviors I have always thought of as "bias for bold action." Perhaps these aren't the ideal employee characteristics from the company's perspective, but they sure helped drive my Great Boss' career. He could readily define a pathway to a better future and wasn't afraid to head down that trail immediately even if he had to drag everyone else along behind him. At times, his "bold actions" upset existing strategies, relationships, and career trajectories. He made enemies. And although he was usually right, he sometimes made mistakes.

His bold actions often angered peers. His bosses were undoubtedly frustrated by him. But everyone grudgingly acknowledged his abilities, and most put up with the resulting disruptions, because he was taking us to somewhere better than where we had been.

As a subordinate, I was inspired. At times, even in awe. I've often heard people debate whether we can become better strategists or if vision is something that is part of our DNA. Is skill in strategy a result of nature or nurture?

After three decades in business, I can confidently conclude it is a bit of both.

What not to do

For a long time, one of my employers was in the thrall of the Gallup Corporation, subscribing to several of their leadership paradigms. One of Gallup's theories at the time was that people are born with certain, innate strengths (which they labeled "talents") and weaknesses. (I'm not sure what they called these.) They further asserted that because of our natural predispositions, talents can only be changed by small amounts through education, training, experience, and personal development efforts.

In the Gallup world, the ability to see potential futures effectively and devise strategies falls into this category of talents. If you have this talent, great. If not, don't waste your time trying to improve in this area, because you'll become frustrated and will be lucky to make any noticeable progress.

At the company level, this means that you shouldn't waste time trying to put into an employee what "God left out." If a particular salesperson lacks a critical ability (such as a talent for quickly developing close, trusting relationships) then he needs to be moved to a different job where the talents he actually possesses will be utilized and those he lacks won't undermine his success.

Or maybe you should just fire him and move on to someone with stronger "relationship talent." Yeah, that would probably be easier – in the Gallup world, anyway.

I found this entire concept to be deflating in the extreme – specifically the notion that if you weren't born with it, you aren't ever going to have it. Nowhere did this theory seem to be truer (at least in the Gallup viewpoint) than in the area of strategy.

A talent for strategy is generally conceded to be critical to success in the most senior roles in a company. If you don't have a strategy talent (they told me mine was middling), you don't belong in the company's most senior roles.

End of story.

I'm afraid I simply don't buy this rather deflating view of human beings.

A case in point

I took a course in strategy in graduate school. Prior to that course, I would have been hard pressed to define "strategy." I didn't really know what people were talking about when the subject came up (nor did many of those in such conversations). I struggled with how to think about

141

strategy, and how to classify it. The course gave me a framework to apply to the subject and plenty of examples (case studies) to illustrate how to apply that framework. As a result, my ability to recognize and devise strategy improved dramatically.

When I went to work for my Great Boss, he taught me much more. He explained his thinking in the development and application of strategy in the real world. And, of course, I had plenty of opportunities to observe his thinking in action. Some plans didn't work, but most did – and truthfully, sometimes a mix of success and failure can be the best teacher.

Today, I consider myself a pretty good strategist – my apologies to Gallup and the entire hour they spent with me to assess all of my talents. Gallup, you're just wrong on this point. And while I might not rise to the strategy-skill level of my Great Boss, I'm far from having "average" capabilities.

Things you should do

The best abilities will be largely wasted if you lack the nerve to implement. A lack of action makes even the best strategies little more than interesting paper exercises. To paraphrase Edison – strategy is 1% inspiration and 99% perspiration.

My best boss was adept at advocating for and applying his strategies, a process he often described as "placing bets." From his perspective, adding value as a senior manager was all about trying new things and making improvements to the business, but he also knew that not everything would work. In most cases, even a perfect strategy requires a cooperative, predictable environment.

He dealt with this by having a multitude of strategies and projects running in parallel. In fact, I saw him set some initiatives in motion on the fly. My best boss had a bias toward taking action as opposed to endless intellectualizing on the subject.

An example

One day the two of us sat in his office for an hour theorizing about other technologies or products the company could add to its portfolio to improve our offering. We were looking for products that would make our customers that much more attached to us as a supplier. After a time, we lit on a diagnostics service and the associated hardware, a new technology that was just coming to the forefront. This new idea was so far afield from where we presently were with our current products that I instantly knew we needed to do further research.

Within a day, I'd located an industry expert and picked his brain. Within a week, another outside expert visited us for a day and assisted us to understand the technology better and also helped us to identify potential acquisition targets. Within another week, we'd made contact with both of the leading companies in the industry and had visits scheduled.

While we never completed a deal in this area (primarily an issue of inadequate customer overlap), the example serves to illustrate my Great Boss' bias toward action. Even as the strategy was gelling, we were already starting to execute. Many of these forays didn't pan out. The few times one did, however, it usually had a big impact. Contrast this approach with the more traditional "analysis paralysis" that occurs with many managers.

Each of these types of initiatives became a part of the overall portfolio of risks in which my Great Boss chose to invest his time. In his mind, this was all about stacking the deck with plenty of good cards so he would always have a chance of drawing some aces.

This was at least in part because he knew some defeats were inevitable.

I benefited by watching how he orchestrated the balancing act. I'd never been reluctant to launch into a project if I thought it held great promise. On my own I would have been more impetuous and much inclined to put all my eggs in one basket. My Great Boss taught me how to think about strategies and their implementation on a grander scale and also how important it was to get the ball rolling quickly.

The bigger picture

Gallup was right about one thing – learning how to take bold action can't be completely learned in a classroom. While you can develop frameworks and ways of thinking in an academic environment, the core learning is experiential – the kind of stuff you need to be in the middle of to understand fully. Strategy and its implementation are full of subtleties and nuances that are hard to tease out from a distance.

Skill in strategy development and an understanding of its implementation, combined with a bias toward action and the perceptiveness to amass a balanced portfolio of risks, are skills take a long time to develop. They are also necessary skills to ensure success as a high-level executive. Even if one doesn't have the ambition or desire to move to a high-level management position, learning how to take bold action makes a job more interesting, exciting, and impactful, resulting in greater job satisfaction.

Because my Great Boss set such a superlative example, I was able to absorb many of these lessons early in my career. I thank my good fortune to have been mentored by a man with such strong skills and a willingness to tutor such a neophyte.

Arguably, this is the most important reason he was my greatest boss.

Chapter 21

An Example of Hard Work

It may seem obvious to most people, but it's hard to inspire your subordinates if you don't "walk the walk" yourself. Over my career, I've seen many bosses chastise employees for a lack of dedication and effort that they, themselves, did not demonstrate. As a boss, you cannot exhibit a weak work ethic and expect your subordinates not to skip out on their obligations at every opportunity.

And by "working hard," I'm referring to both taking on the difficult tasks and putting in the hours. Skimp in either category and you're just asking for sneers as soon as your back is turned.

What not to do

I've had a couple of bosses that consistently worked less than a forty-hour week. One of these bosses loved being on the golf course and took every opportunity to play. Sometimes she justified her absences by claiming her recreational activity had a "business purpose," while other times she was guilty of simply ducking out of the office when the weather was cooperative and she thought no one was watching (but someone is always watching). She may have thought herself clever, but all her subordinates knew exactly what was happening. We all understood the game she was playing. And we all figuratively flipped her off anytime she urged one of us to put in an extra effort.

Fortunately for her, that boss rarely took shots at her subordinates over their work hours, because doing so would have represented the height of hypocrisy.

An example

I remember one day when the golfer's boss called me, demanding to know where the absentee manager might be found. Apparently, the big boss had been trying to reach her for hours (this was before the age of cell phones), and supposedly nobody knew her whereabouts. I was well aware of her movements – as undoubtedly, were my peers in the department. As usual, she was playing 18 on a nearby course.

At that moment, I was faced with a tough choice. I could fib and cover for the boss, a lazy buffoon who was a poster child for the Peter Principle (promoted beyond her capabilities). Or I could answer honestly and expose her.

In this case, I lied to the big boss. I could easily fob off my response as "misplaced loyalty," but when I'm honest with myself, I have to admit I was simply afraid to cross someone higher and potentially more powerful than I. Today – older and much more politically savvy – I would likely do things differently. In retrospect, I find this entire incident to be a problem not because I lied to the big boss, but because it made me resent my supervisor for putting me in the position in the first place. In fact, I found myself feeling like he owed me rather than the other way around, even though he never really knew about the incident.

A second, similar example

A little later in my career, I experienced another boss who was frequently absent from the office. In this case, no one on the team was aware of where she was going or why. Not surprisingly, this led to endless speculation. Was she having an affair? Seeing her psychiatrist? Planning a hostile takeover of the company?

The speculation grew wilder each time she was inexplicably absent.

Of course, no one in this workgroup felt compelled to put in any kind of extraordinary effort – why should we subject ourselves to all that pressure when our leader clearly didn't do so herself? When she was absent, in fact, the effort level would drop off noticeably, and some of the less mature employees would engage in practical jokes and other unauthorized shenanigans.

Eventually, I discovered this boss had some personal issues that drew her away from the office. I never inquired exactly what this entailed – never wanted to know, quite frankly. Had she been more forthright with her subordinates, we would have been more sympathetic. Probably even the least dedicated among us would have goofed off less. At least, until she started giving her people "the business" over their work habits.

Bottom line, if you don't "walk the talk," you won't have any credibility when "talking the talk."

A great boss

My great boss was in the office a lot. While he rarely beat me to the door in the morning, as I'm an early riser, he was often in the office well past the end of my day. I never had any doubts that he was working at least as hard as I was. Probably harder, in fact. I later found the example he set was important to my managerial development in three ways.

First, he was communicating the importance of hard work to me through his actions (and with words, as well). If I wanted to get ahead, I needed to devote more than a basic 40 hours per week to the effort. And I also needed to go above and beyond the basics of my job description to take on the toughest problems that the business faced. Basically, I needed to focus my work in a way to impress the "higher ups."

Second, as the strength of his work ethic became well known across the company, I began to recognize the grudging respect it commanded among his peers and with his boss. Even though "results count, not effort," most people value managers who put in the kind of sweat needed to get those results. That applies even when things aren't going particularly well. Hard work can carry you through lean times. Rather than eye rolls, he earned back slaps.

Third, the longer-than-normal work hours became a part of our shared experience together as boss-subordinate. There is nothing like a bilateral sacrifice to help people work together for a common goal. There is no doubt in my mind that the resulting comradery helped him open up to me on sensitive and politically charged issues, at least much sooner in our relationship that would have otherwise occurred.

Working hard was a lesson I've tried to apply throughout my years as a manager.

Another example – "that damned strategy conference"

One important event that happened each year while I worked for my great boss was the companywide strategy conference. For those of us in or close to corporate headquarters, this was a pivotal "shared pain" experience. Business groups handled aggregating the individual strategies of their component divisions and turning this agglomeration into something coherent and persuasive.

It was tough work and typically required postulating new, high-risk ideas and selling those concepts to the most senior manager within the business unit. Getting this right was critically important (as it was a rare occasion to make a positive impression on the company's CEO and his immediate staff). Yet despite the high stakes, I never saw my Great Boss give any ground on what he believed to be the right path in an effort to be more politically correct.

In the final few days before the conference, we pulled together the overarching strategies and constructed PowerPoint slides to convey and justify the core ideas. Dry runs were intense at this stage, and tempers were often short as time was running short. My Great Boss worked alongside me, helping to craft the message and manipulate the reams of data. He was a participant rather than a detractor standing on the sidelines lobbing critiques (which is what most of the company's senior managers seemed to do when the pressure was high).

At the end of the process, I owned the strategy as much as my boss and the senior business unit executive. It was the perfect way (painful though it might be in terms of long, hard hours) to make sure we were all on the same page.

The bigger picture

Great bosses "walk the talk" as well as they "talk the talk," and nowhere is this more evident than in their dedication to getting things accomplished through hard work. Certainly hard work means putting in the hours, but it also means staying in the middle of difficult and undesirable tasks. When the boss is willing to roll up her sleeves and dive in with the rest of the team, she enhances her credibility, cultivates loyalty, and sets a positive example for her subordinates.

While early in my career, I found myself snickering over the weak effort of an absentee boss. Later, I felt downright irate when a boss' hypocrisy surfaced. My Great Boss never failed to put in at least as much effort as his most dedicated subordinate. Draining though it may have been, my Great Boss' work ethic could only be described as "inspirational."

Chapter 22

Regulating One's Temper

Most of us have a temper. We get angry. Things in the corporate world frustrate us – dumb decisions, laziness, obvious political pandering, senseless directives. The list is almost limitless. When we are angry, we're tempted to act out, handing a little piece of our annoyance to everyone that is even remotely involved (and often innocent bystanders, as well).

Most of us eventually learn it is important to keep our tempers in check. We roll our eyes and shake our heads. We walk away. We have a pet phrase that we repeat over and over to soothe our frayed nerves. Alas, the effort doesn't always come with complete success. Mastery of one's temper is a part of acting like an adult. And we all know the potential consequences of a lost temper – embarrassment, lost friendships, new and unexpected enemies, and in extreme instances even violence.

We all try to learn to manage our tempers like big boys and girls.

Unless we happen to be the boss. When the boss is angry, all bets are off. Many bosses seem to feel that subordinates need, or even want, to see them display their tempers. They act as if they are entitled to their rage. And seemingly, the bigger the boss, the bigger potential for him to become a gigantic, temperamental jerk.

As human beings, we are all occasionally roiled by our emotions, but as the boss, we can use those emotions as an excuse to punish subordinates, or channel the energy in a way that doesn't victimize others.

What not to do – the Screamers

The most obvious type of ill-tempered manager is the Screamer, a behavioral type I discussed in the first half of this book. I've had a couple of these bosses over the years and observed plenty of others. Screamers do exactly what the name says – they scream. And while I've seen Screamers go after peers, suppliers, and even customers, mostly they direct their vitriol at their subordinates.

Usually, a Screamer revs up with a raised voice before going into complete meltdown. Once you hear the volume begin to rise, watch out. The escalation of both decibels and vehemence can happen very quickly with a screamer. In fact, in many cases, a full rant may be impossible to stop once the cycle has started. When you are on the receiving end of a tirade, there are only a few options – sit back and take it, fight back, or try to be the voice of reason in a hurricane of emotion.

I've observed that fighting back seems to be a more successful way of handling this type of temper attack than the passive approaches. I'm not talking about a perfunctory objection, however. I mean giving back as much as you are taking.

An example

I once observed a classic Screamer (and in this case a CEO to boot, so there were very few, if any, limits placed on his behavior by others in the organization) go after one of my subordinates during a presentation. The CEO was standing on the balls of his feet, screaming obscenities in a bombastic voice as his face turned from bright red to purple. I'd seen this scenario from this man a dozen times. I knew exactly where it was headed – to a ten-minute diatribe where the subordinate was reduced to mush as the CEO harshly passed judgment over every element of his work.

And that was exactly what happened.

The incident was caused by this subordinate blithely claiming that he had cut his department's budget. The statement wasn't part of his rehearsed remarks and was not supported by the data included as backup materials. The CEO pounced, flaying the man in front of me, my boss, the head of the business unit, and every one of his peers.

Later, in a closed session with my HR manager, the CEO said he "…was not at all confident in that guy." I understood this as an instruction to get rid of him, and a couple days later he was cleaning out his desk.

Had he stood up to the CEO, he might have had a chance of keeping his job. Instead, the Screamer immediately classified the manager as a "weakling," and that was all it took to start his ouster.

What not to do – The Grudge-holders

The other type of temperamental boss I've dealt with is much harder to identify, and his mood is much more difficult to assess. This boss – I'll call him the "Grudge-holder" – outwardly keeps his temper in check but smolders inside as he carefully calculates the weight and gravity of an offending party's transgressions.

He never forgets. Apparently for the Grudge-holder, such offenses never seem to dissipate with time.

Given the right opportunity, the Grudge-holder will exact revenge when the target is most vulnerable. And then he will pounce, taking his pound of flesh while proving that at least for him, revenge is a dish best served cold.

It is bad enough when a Grudge-holding peer has you in his sights, but when it is a boss (and particularly, a CEO), you are living your corporate life on borrowed time.

Another example

I observed one CEO hold a grudge against two subordinates that extended in time to several years, even though both men had long since left the company. The animus was only satisfied when the pair ended up forced into selling their own, post-corporate startup. This particular Grudge-holder was so image-conscious that he was forced to delay seeking revenge until doing so presented no threat to his reputation.

In this situation, the two subordinates labored for roughly five years while at the company to develop a new product for a new market the company wished to enter. For a variety of reasons (which are too complicated to go into here), the effort failed. Not only did the employees fail, the CEO decided that these two men had intentionally misled him to keep the project going long after it should have been shut down. In fact, he was quite incensed about it. Undoubtedly, the Grudge-holder being more than once forced into a position where he was sticking his neck out with board members over the project had something to do with his ire.

He hid his emotions well, but I later learned that he was so furious with the two subordinates that he was quietly marking time and hoping for a chance to exact revenge. I personally had my doubts about the CEO's conclusion – that the pair had intentionally misled him. At the time, nobody wanted to believe in the project more than these two guys. When their errors were laid at their feet, they continued to be in denial – true believers in the project and cause.

Eventually, the project was shut down, and the two employees (and some others) were terminated. Then the pair did something completely unexpected – they started their own, new company to produce a variation of the design we had rejected.

The Grudge-holder seethed. A few months later, I suggested that I negotiate a license with the two for all our intellectual property in the space. I reasoned that since we clearly weren't going to use it, if they were the least bit successful, we might be able to recover a small portion of the money we'd lost in our doomed market-entry effort. You'd have thought I suggested the boss give up his first born.

It quickly became apparent that there was no way the CEO was going to license anything to these two "traitors," no matter what the price and terms. In fact, I could tell he would have loved nothing more than to find an opportunity to pursue them in court, where the larger corporation's deeper pockets would overwhelm the tiny startup. We only lacked a good pretense, something a potential patent violation could provide.

That's grudge-holding. It can be ugly when you see up close and personal.

As it turned out, the company was right, and the pair of subordinates-turned-entrepreneurs were wrong. Their company never amounted to much of anything. And while the CEO missed the opportunity to excoriate the pair in a court of law, he undoubted experienced great satisfaction over their ultimate failure.

My great boss

I'm sure my Great Boss also had a temper just like the rest of us mortals. He was, however, able to manage it far better than most. I saw him frustrated at times. In fact, saw him irate over dumb decisions, unreasonable restrictions, and the inability of others to grasp his point.

But I never saw him personalize it. I never saw him take out his anger on a subordinate. And he definitely never resorted to Grudge-holding and time-delayed revenge.

He somehow managed to process all those emotions and to let his frustrations go.

"I'm not interested in who shot John."

I heard that quote many times. It represented the commitment my Great Boss made to figuring out and fixing the causes of frustrations and failures, rather than fixing a person's name to disasters and subsequently punishing them for their supposed transgressions. I don't know if he was born with an unusual ability to govern his emotional states or if he learned it over many years of dealing with irritating people. I do know that he rarely tried to fix blame. As a result, I never feared opening up, relaying bad news, disagreeing, or even tossing out a half-formed idea once in a while. My Great Boss would never use one of those common sources of irritation as an excuse to take his anger out on me.

An example

During my time with my Great Boss, he found himself in a pitched battle with one of his peers. The subject matter of the dispute was the way forward in a complex and complicated strategy we were pursuing in an attempt to displace an industry leader from their dominant market position. My boss recommended a rapid approach to rolling out the strategy while his peer favored a slower, more deliberate rollout that would ensure that all ducks were in a row.

To help make sure he carried the day, the other executive resorted to the politicking of both their mutual boss as well as other key opinion leaders within the business unit. Ultimately, the battle ended up in a compromise between their two viewpoints.

My boss could have ranted and raved about his opponent. He could have attempted a similar campaign of undermining and politicking. He could have even set traps for his peer, hoping to exact revenge while carrying the day.

He did none of that.

While his lack of response might be seen by some as a sign of weakness, I knew it came from strength. My boss was fully vested in the battle, but not in destroying his opponent. His strict policy of not personalizing his anger and not attempting to carry out revenge is undoubtedly what led to him at least getting half of what he wanted.

The bigger picture

While pundits and poets have often pointed out, "Revenge is a dish that is best served cold," my Great Boss taught me that revenge has no place in a business environment. Nor does screaming, ranting, foaming at the mouth, or other emotionally charged responses to seeing something you don't like. All of these reactions act to limit openness and increase risk aversion in one's subordinates, which ultimately lessens the organization's potential to achieve the best results.

Employees are not looking for an irrational battlefield where they can go toe-to-toe with peers and bosses in an attempt to win lopsided emotional battles. They want facts, rationality, and even-handed rules. A boss that understands this and keeps his emotions under control has the potential to be a Great Boss.

Chapter 23

Taking the Heat

Whether you work for a successful company or one that is struggling, there will always be plenty of blame to go around. As discussed in Chapter 7, many organizations seem to be obsessed with the "search for the guilty, and the punishment of the innocent." If you find yourself in the path of such a witch hunt, you're usually in deep trouble.

Unless you've got protection.

One of the most helpful things my Great Boss did was to step in front of speeding political bullets, effectively shielding me and his other subordinates from the vagaries of the "blame game." Doing this took a high level of commitment to his team. It also took a keen insight into where things might be headed when the assignment of guilt was in its formative stage. And most of all it took guts.

In the present era, we sometimes hear about a manager "throwing someone under the bus." My Great Boss stood in front of the bus, preventing it from running over any of us.

And yes, sometimes he did get hurt as a result.

What not to do

The antithesis of taking the heat is making sure the heat is taken by someone else.

In *Navigating Corporate Politics*, I've written extensively about the practice of scapegoating. In short, scapegoating is the intentional lining up of a victim to take the fall for a "problem project" or "risky strategy." Usually, the technique is not employed malevolently as a tool of revenge, although there is a certain ugly calculus that can take place where the scapegoating manager carefully weighs whom she can most readily sacrifice. It is basically a survival tool, used by unprincipled managers simply to protect their own backsides. I personally find it to be among the most morally repugnant of political tactics, but grudgingly acknowledge that it works.

In fact, I've seen it work quite effectively.

An example

My boss once appointed a general manager for a risky new product development project just as the effort was reaching the critical stage of customer testing. On the surface, the appointment made sense – the project had reached a point where it required more than the technical resources previously managing it. This was a high-risk time for the project, where it needed to transition from concept to the production line, and the appointment of a seasoned GM was the next logical step.

As it turned out, that was only part of the reason for appointing the GM, a fact which became obvious to me when I heard who got the job.

The employee hired as the GM had been on the boss' "dislike" list for a very long time. My boss had previously conducted a campaign to get me to remove this particular employee a few years earlier when she reported to me – a job she appeared to be handling quite well at the time. The reasons are too complicated to go into here, but suffice it to say the boss simply favored someone else for that job. When I was transferred to another division, the GM only lasted a few months under my replacement before she was put in a staff position, her wheels spinning.

I thought this manager was headed out the door – I advised her to leave, in fact – but instead she eventually ended up heading this risky development project. The reason was clear – she would be an obvious sacrificial lamb if the project didn't pan out.

And, as you can probably guess, it didn't. When things went sideways, the GM was the one that delivered the bad news. She was in the front seat, taking the heat from the rest of the management team and the board of directors. When the project was eliminated, she (along with two other senior people in engineering and sales) was fired.

I don't know how my boss explained this to the board, but I can guess....

Something else to avoid

Most bosses aren't scapegoaters, but they are sometimes guilty of dodging bullets in an attempt to protect their own posteriors – often to the detriment of their subordinates.

For a capable boss, no major project or initiative develops in a vacuum. The boss is typically involved in the process in an intimate way, and if she isn't, then shame on her. In short – any project coming from a boss' area of responsibility technically belongs to *her*. She owns it. Even if she neglects the details and delegates the broad strokes. Even if her subordinate runs far out ahead of her. There should be no escape from this reality.

Except many bosses successfully duck and dodge.

When things start to go sideways, the mediocre boss knows to agree with those higher up while heaping blame on one of his subordinates. This is typically done by piling on to already accumulating condemnation, or through the simple unwillingness to step in on the subordinate's behalf.

Another example

I recall an instance where I failed to protect a hapless subordinate in just this fashion.

At a strategy review meeting, one of my subordinates made a rash overstatement during her portion of the presentation – something to the effect that even though one of the technical staff members had "invented most of our key products," she was demoting the man.

It was a dumb thing to say. We hadn't actually made a change in the technical manager's assignment. Instead, we'd simply brought in another manager with better people skills to handle the managerial tasks. By the time of this review, it probably "felt like" she'd been demoted, but no change in salary or status had actually taken place.

The CEO, the one with the bad temper from the previous chapter, immediately latched onto this error. She then proceeded to torture my subordinate for a good ten minutes, including screaming at her over the "stupidity" of the statement. I should have stepped in front of that speeding freight train, but I didn't. I was terrified by the CEO's behavior and wanted nothing to do with the incident.

My Great Boss would have given better to his subordinate. Yep, I was chicken. But I learned a lesson that day and tried to do better in the future.

A great boss

Perhaps it was an outgrowth of his maturity and the presence of "walk away" money, but my Great Boss never left a subordinate twisting in the wind.

By this point in his career, he had already served as the CEO of a substantial company and had enough savings that he didn't have to worry about collecting the next paycheck. But I doubt either of these things was a major factor when it came to how he treated his employees. He was still as achievement oriented as anyone I'd ever known and was far from "coasting" out his final years before retirement.

Still, he didn't have to protect us. He did so because, in his view of work and management, it was the right thing to do. I know he was unusually brave, being unwilling to let one of "his people" take unwarranted or excessive criticism. I believe that partially explained his willingness to step in front of the bus, but I've always seen more to it that just that.

Personal loyalty. That was the extra factor. His special sauce. My best boss was committed to our little team in a way that was unusual by today's corporate standards. And while it might have exposed him to potential political problems, he did a good job managing those risks by staying close to the projects we worked on and watching how we interacted with those above us.

Yes, my Great Boss realized that loyalty was a two-way street. By showing his loyalty to us, he earned loyalty back with interest. His demonstration of loyalty had side benefits – like getting me to work harder for him than any other boss to whom I ever reported.

A final example

I remember an incident where one of my peers was in front of a large crowd (including the COO, but not the company's vitriolic CEO) giving a presentation on pricing. When the questioning became heated and my peer faltered – as always seemed to happen at this company – my Great Boss stepped into the gap. I remember him saying, "If you have a problem with pricing policy, you need to talk to ME, not my analyst."

And they did "talk" to him. In attack mode. For what seemed like forever. Of course, my boss was much better than I would have been (and also much better than the peer who was on the ropes) at taking on the pointed interrogation. He fought back appropriately, and in the end, nobody got hurt.

My peer would have probably suffered a major career setback had not our mutual boss intervened.

The bigger picture

A Great Boss doesn't leave her subordinates exposed and unprotected when there are problems. A part of the "loyalty deal" she has with her people includes an unspoken willingness to step in and take the heat when things haven't gone well. Doing so takes plenty of intestinal fortitude, but it produces benefits over the longer haul, and not only for the protected employees but for the boss and the overall organization.

Lesser managers step away from their subordinates, or even sometimes offer up employees as a "corporate sacrifice" when a particular failure appears to demand one. While such managers may protect themselves in the short term, they give up the positive relationships, loyalty, and higher levels of performance a Great Boss commands.

Chapter 24

Credibility

Unlike most of the other qualities demonstrated by my greatest boss, credibility is something that wasn't inside of him. Credibility is a judgment granted by others. It comes about as your boss' peers, superiors, and the organization in general, recognize talent and realize that with his presence, the company performs better than it would without him.

Perhaps he has an unparalleled technical skill. Or perhaps his track record is beyond reproach. His credibility might even be a result of piercing insight or a towering intellect. The point is that without credibility, your boss' ability to help you is severely undermined, regardless of his other great characteristics.

A great boss

When it came to my Great Boss, the granting of credibility came about as a result of his superlative qualities. Things such as his ability to understand and develop strategy, his inspiring work ethic, his willingness to step in front of the bus rather than letting it run over people, and his willingness to take bold action. All of these characteristics made him credible in the eyes of his boss and our CEO.

There was also an element credibility that came from his past accomplishments. My Great Boss had once been a CEO himself. He'd been fired from that job a short time after the company was sold to a foreign-owned firm, one that just could not seem to tolerate his "maverick" ways. Not only did he have the title, but the CEO job he held was with a significant and respected competitor. Even his peers inside of our company were grudgingly forced to acknowledge his time as a CEO was skillfully executed.

Credibility gave him... space. It generated an automatic respect response. It gave him enough leeway to operate in the way he needed to be a Great Boss. He took advantage of the leeway by letting his subordinates take risks and had plenty of capacity to take the heat when if and when things didn't work out as planned.

This reputation was an essential part of his success as a boss. It was essential for some of his other great characteristics to shine. As a result of his credibility, he was able to take more and bigger (but still measured) risks. He was able to give me more opportunities to fail because the impact on his own reputation would likely be less. To a degree, he was Teflon-coated.

An example

I had a brief consultation with the company's President before he brought in my Great Boss. Before that, I had been directly reporting to the President, but with the hiring of this "new guy," I was told that would change. I would be reporting to the new guy rather than the President – a change I initially reacted to in a negative way.

I recall the President said that my new boss was "...expensive, but he knows the industry as well as anyone, and he has a great reputation as a strategist. He should be able to make a big difference in developing our plans to defeat Competitor X."

Of course, he didn't say "Competitor X," but the picture was clear – my Great Boss walked in the door having instant credibility with top management. At that point it was his to lose – he would either enhance it with a demonstration of his abilities or quickly convince everyone that he wasn't really performing at the level of his reputation.

You already know which way it went.

There is no doubt my Great Boss began his work with the company with more freedom to act than the average manager, and this was based on his sterling reputation alone. And while he likely would have still been my greatest supervisor if he hadn't had this amazing credibility, it further enhanced his other skills and abilities.

What not to do

There are numerous things that can damage credibility – a failed project, a stupid statement made off-the-cuff, politicking against a rival, even a gaff made during a presentation. Credibility takes a thousand successful actions to build, but only one mistake to damage. In some organizations, a single highly visible slip up can cause a downward slide.

The answer to building and maintaining credibility is simple – superior performance, a stellar reputation coming into the firm, and no major miscues.

Easier said than done.

Another example

In one of my general management jobs, I hired a specialist to manage a series of small businesses reporting to me. The specialist had an excellent track record coming into the company and a compelling vision of how he would pull the small businesses together into a cohesive unit while adding a few "bolt-on" acquisitions.

Then he had a chance meeting with my boss.

Alas, I wasn't present during this discussion, but I understood from an observer that the specialist stumbled over a few financial terms. (He was somewhat weak in this area, but accounting acumen wasn't why I hired him.) This single incident blew his credibility with my superior and resulted in my boss applying continual, low-grade pressure for me to remove him.

When you have no "boss cred," you're tentative. You can't easily advance your strategies and ideas. People don't listen to you. You have a tough time defending your subordinates. Almost everything is more difficult.

My subordinate experienced all these problems.

He was a good boss, and his people were loyal and enjoyed working for him. But his damaged credibility meant he would never be a Great Boss, at least not at that company.

Credibility enhances a manager's ability to execute several of the "Great Boss" skills I've written about in this book. For example, career management assistance is much more effective if the boss' judgment is trusted by those above him. Taking bold actions may only be possible in many organizations if you have the confidence of your superiors. In general, the more credibility, the greater the possible risks that can be undertaken. Providing subordinates with chances to fail pretty much only happens when the boss feels "secure," a state which normally also requires credibility.

That's why I've often said: "If you want to work for a Great Boss, look for someone that has the confidence of his boss and those further up the ladder." While a boss still fighting to establish himself can be good, likely there will be deficiencies – particularly when those things might put his fledgling reputation at risk.

Yet another example

Early in my career, I worked as an engineer on a newly installed production line. My assignment was to use a camera to direct a robot to locate, pick up, and place a product it in a fixture. While describing the objective is easy, a high degree of product mix resulted in there being quite a few technical hurdles to successful implementation.

There was a backup plan, an expensive mechanical orientation system that we knew would work. It would cost more, run slower, and take up a lot more floor space than the robotic solution. When we reached a decision point and had to go one way or the other, I hadn't worked out all the bugs with my approach, although I was sure those issues could be solved.

My boss, one of my better ones, went with the mechanical system despite my confidence that I would succeed with the robotic solution. It wasn't until years later that I realized he lacked the credibility to sell my solution unless it were already working perfectly. Additionally, he didn't have the reputation to come through unscathed if there were a failure on my part. My approach was too risky – for him.

Had I been working for my Great Boss, I have little doubt he would have approved the preferred approach.

And had the project been successful, it would have represented a nice boost to my career – and my credibility.

A final example

While I had worked on a couple of acquisitions before working for my Great Boss (in minor roles), I'd never run the show. When my Great Boss asked me if I'd like to take the lead in negotiating one, I was eager to do so.

It was quite some time before I realized what a big risk he was taking by putting me in charge.

I found myself talking pricing and terms with the founder of the business, a man twice my age with oodles more experience. Somehow, with the assistance of my boss, I managed to persevere through this stage. I coordinated the contract drafting. I headed up the due diligence process. I even defined and coordinated (for a time) the integration of the target company.

The experience was invaluable, but I can't help but think that putting me in charge took a rather large leap of faith. My Great Boss, however, specialized in putting me in "learning situations," and this one became one of the biggest of my career.

In hindsight, I realized he could only do this because he knew his credibility was rock solid with his boss and those higher in the company (including the CEO). Those people accepted his judgment – even if he put a "kid" in charge of a small but important deal.

As it turned out, I didn't screw up anything too badly. (Kudos to my boss for redirecting me a couple of times just before I walked off the edge of a cliff.) The deal ended up successfully closing. Last time I checked, it appeared that it had been relatively easily integrated into the mother ship and was performing well.

The bigger picture

While a supervisor's personal credibility doesn't directly affect the boss-subordinate relationship, it definitely governs how far a boss can go when working to develop an employee. Because of his substantial credibility, my greatest boss was able to take me further in my career faster than any other boss I've ever had.

While a boss can be "good" without credibility, to be truly "great" (from a subordinate's perspective) credibility granting the freedom to act independently is an absolute necessity.

Chapter 25

Friendship

When I was learning to supervise others, I often received advice about how I should "keep my distance" when it came to friendships. After years of experience as a manager, I've come to realize this is something of a mindless mantra that deserves to be challenged. The apparent logic of this bit of management wisdom is that emotional detachment allows for greater objectivity and won't result in any hesitation to discipline or even terminate when necessary. And it avoids favoritism, real or perceived.

I have come to realize that such logic does a great disservice to employees and managers alike.

As a manager, I found it nearly impossible to spend 40+ hours with my subordinates every week and not develop an emotional attachment to at least a few of them. Sure, a few subordinates engender a sense of dispassionate detachment by being jerks. They turn out to be the kind of person you wouldn't want to befriend in a hundred years. Most, I've learned, are good people of the type worthy of a closer relationship. And while there is no need for the boss to become their "best friend at work" (a nod to Gallup for this concept, a part of their famous Q12 survey), there's also absolutely no need to be standoffish.

You shouldn't be afraid of attachment. In fact, where I've allowed friendships to develop with a few of my subordinates, the awkwardness and emotional trauma of managing future problems (terminations or discipline) has actually been reduced.

An example of what not to do

One of my early supervisors provided a good template of the conventional thinking when it comes to boss-subordinate relationships. She isolated herself from her direct reports and maintained a gruff exterior, one that made her seem completely unapproachable. She had a couple of "back-slap and laugh" friendships with peers – ones that seemed quite superficial. Her peers were also competitors, at least when it came to moving further up the ladder. The tension caused by this rivalry would have made developing real friendships quite difficult. Her own boss clearly set the tone by being as distant as she was.

Work couldn't have been a lot of fun for him.

True friendships in the work environment involve casual time spent together for reasons other than a strict business purpose. A degree of mutual disclosure is normally present, including revelations that expose a person to some degree of risk if the "friend" turns out to be a faker. Alas, this is not an uncommon occurrence in relationships between work peers.

In reality, most "work friendships" are "friendships of convenience." Such relationships have little depth to them and are entered into and terminated based on whom an employee is physically around on a regular basis and who might prove to be "useful" in the immediate future – a little like an alliance on a reality show, which you know will end at some point, but not when or how.

My boss acted pretty much as you would expect from an adherent to conventional wisdom – she was distant, a bit cold, and was quick to offer biting criticism when she didn't approve of how one was approaching a project or problem. I found the woman hard to like, impossible to love, and definitely less than inspiring when it came to rallying the group or leading us toward a common goal.

Did my effort suffer as a result? I must admit the answer is "not much." I was young, full of enthusiasm for my job, and would have labored hard for anyone at that point. This boss might have been better able to direct my energies with a little more congeniality and a lot less critique. Despite the small amount of adversity, I was still willing to work hard for the perceived future reward of "getting ahead."

I can't say the same for my peers, however. Two of them actively disliked the boss and took every opportunity to mock and undermine her when her back was turned. This eventually spilled over to others, as the pair were happy to supply negative comments and observations to any of the boss' detractors (primarily others in management). A third peer simply tried to keep as far away from this hypercritical boss as possible, handling assignments as if he reported to no one most of the time. This led to decisions that were sometimes at odds with the company's larger objectives.

My conclusion (reached years later): "Keeping her distance" substantially undermined this boss' career potential.

Another bad example

Another boss I had many years later had a completely different approach to handling relationships with subordinates – she faked them.

This boss was much higher on the management ladder than the first supervisor I described, and she'd learned a few tricks of the trade along the way. By nature, she was a person very aware of her image. Over the years, she had developed a carefully constructed mask that she presented to practically everyone in the company. She used this to protect her reputation as a generous and easy-to-work-for boss. When one interacted with her, it was almost always with the mask and rarely with the real person beneath.

On the surface, she was friendly, welcoming, engaging, and outgoing. I heard people outside of the company remark what a "great boss" she must be. She appeared to be open to the kind of friendship I knew from experience could make work a pleasure rather than a dull chore.

But appearances were far from the truth. It took a few months of direct interaction, but I eventually realized there was an alter ego under the surface, one that was introverted, impatient, a harsh judge, and vindictive. And while her normal demeanor was pleasant enough, there were times she accidentally let her guard down and the real, vicious politician made an appearance.

There could be no authentic friendship with this creature – at least not if you worked for her. Our "mutual" disclosure was strictly one direction, and anything you said would definitely be used against you if it served her purposes.

I grew to loathe working for this executive, and I wasn't alone. Even though relationships between peers are often tentative in the work environment – and particularly difficult when the atmosphere is politically charged, as this one was – I eventually discovered that all my peers also disliked her. Some even held the woman in complete contempt despite a high level of achievement and an obvious, great intelligence.

The cold, distant relationship had several noticeable impacts on my performance. Misgivings of the boss and her motives led me to be suspicious of my peers. The tone at the top created an environment ripe for political maneuvering, and my peers and I often found ourselves working at cross-purposes. I disliked interacting with the boss so much that I tended to keep things to myself – even things that rightfully should have been brought to her attention. This worked to my detriment on more than one occasion. And there was never any doubt that she was willing to "throw people under the bus" if outcomes were anything less than what was demanded – no matter how unreasonable.

Ultimately, there was a high rate of turnover within her group of subordinates, although admittedly as much of it a result of her own political maneuvering and expectations of perfection as voluntary quits.

A great boss

By contrast, my Great Boss became a true friend – without qualification or subterfuge. Contrary to conventional wisdom, he had no fear of drawing close to his subordinates. I detected no fakery in his manner – no "man behind the curtain." Instead, he was 100% authentic in his interactions with me and, as far as I could tell, with his other subordinates.

His authenticity included an ability to engage in the progressive mutual disclosure normally exhibited by friends. As a result, I learned his opinion about those above him in the company, and he understood my career ambitions as well as my strengths and limitations. We spent time together outside of work, and our families got to know each other (despite a substantial difference in age and position in life). I had never experienced this kind of friendship before – at least not at work – and I responded positively to it by working harder than I ever had in my life.

I looked forward to coming to the office each day. When I was able to collaborate on something with my boss, it was even better. Without the friendship, I suspect I would have benefited far less from all the other great qualities he brought to the table. Friendship opened me up to a greater degree of learning.

He maintained friendly relations with most of his subordinates. Some of his former direct reports, who were scattered throughout our company and other firms in the industry (his relationships with them having been established earlier in their careers when they'd both worked elsewhere), helped him with intelligence gathering and guiding the organization's strategy. Without relationships that involved deep trust and respect, he would have never been able to tap such knowledge and ultimately achieve some of the big successes he managed.

I never saw him betrayed by any of these friends. Not even once. Nor did I ever see him shrink from the friendships despite the fact that he sometimes had to make unpleasant calls when it came to their job assignments or careers.

A final example

As I noted at the beginning of this chapter, the biggest objection most people offer to close boss-subordinate friendships is that they interfere with making "tough calls."

I can assure you that hasn't been the case, at least not as far as my personal experience goes.

After my working for my Great Boss, I began actively cultivating friendships with my subordinates. While I was never as good at it as he was, I ended up with some relationships that survived departures from companies (mine or the subordinate's). Today, I find those friendships to be a comfort and a source of great enjoyment.

In one instance (of several that have occurred over the years), I was called upon to make a deep cut in employment because of an unexpected economic downturn. This included terminating two people on my direct staff.

One of the two I selected (based solely on business needs) was a close friend, the other not so much. I actually found it much easier to let the friend go. She completely understood the economic situation as a result of our previous conversations on the subject. As a result, we were able to have a calm, rational discussion about how to make her transition out of the firm as easy as possible. While it was far from pleasant, we worked through the situation, and our friendship survived the traumatic event.

The other employee had been cultivating her own relationship, but in her case, it was with *my* boss. As a result, she seemed to think of herself as "untouchable." She was caught completely unaware when I let her know she was being terminated. She was angry, bitter, and ended up losing her temper. Needless to say, we didn't sort out any kind of "smooth transition." The entire episode was emotionally draining, and for years afterward, this former subordinate was angry with me.

Odds are these exact circumstances would not be repeated again, but the incident was an instructive illustration of the difference between firing friends and those that are held at a distance. While it might seem counterintuitive, it has been my experience that a close relationship makes implementing the "tough call" easier, no matter what the employee's predisposition might be.

The bigger picture

Friendships between a boss and her subordinates can be tricky to manage. While they undoubtedly help the manager get the most she can from her subordinates, and they contribute to a more pleasant and positive work experience, friendships can open up the boss to perceptions of favoritism. Favoritism, much like unfairness, can be quite destructive to the morale of a work group. The manager that befriends her subordinates needs to be aware of any treatment that might be seen by others as inequitable.

Another risk of friendship is something that I call "strutting." Strutting is when an employee who believes that their special relationship with the boss makes them bullet-proof uses that relationship as leverage to get their way with other employees. This only happens occasionally, but when it does it can also severely damage morale. Fortunately, the solution is simple – a short conversation with the strutter will normally set things right.

Despite these risks, I firmly believe that work friendships are a key to being a Great Boss. They open subordinates up to greater learning and inspire greater commitment than relationships that are strictly at arm's length. My friendship with my Great Boss was the pivotal element that made working for him the best superior-subordinate experience of my career.

Chapter 26

Conclusion

This brings us to the end of my exploration of supervisory excellence. My apologies for the necessary overlap in some subjects – sometimes it is hard to draw a sharp line between characteristics like "explaining the rationale behind important decisions" and "communicating the 'big picture.'" While I would have preferred to have avoided any overlap in subjects, I felt there was enough nuance in each category to justify breaking it out separately.

Pulling it all together

Eleven chapters on avoiding common managerial failure modes. Fourteen chapters illustrating what a Great Boss looks like and how to get the skills right. So what does it all mean?

Simply reading the book will not make you a Great Boss – the lessons must be put into action.

I recommend the first step being a serious soul searching. As an aspiring or even an experienced boss, you should determine:

- Do I really care about being a Great Boss, particularly knowing that it doesn't necessarily guarantee my climb up the corporate ladder?
- Which extreme managerial characteristics am I most likely to exhibit?
- Am I already marching down the path toward becoming an extreme manager?
- Which of the "Great Boss" behaviors will be the easiest for me to implement?
- Which will be the hardest?
- Are there any foundational items (a strong track record of performance, a solid work ethic, emotional intelligence, etc.) that I need to work on to adopt some of the Great Boss behaviors?
- Are there any Great Boss behaviors that simply won't work in my organization? Am I sure that I'm not just chickening out of implementing a difficult one?

Once you have a handle on how you want this material to work for you, the next step is to get help where you need it. Perhaps your self-awareness is low (a common characteristic of all employees). If so, a 360-degree review might help. Or perhaps a skills evaluation. Better yet, how about having a heart-to-heart with a former subordinate that knows you well and won't pull punches.

While I'm not generally a big fan of trying to plan a major change in your supervisory style, I do think that selecting certain core skills to focus on over a 3-6 month time horizon, along with frequent self-evaluation, isn't a bad idea.

Test. Experiment. Take some risks in the way you interact with your people, but also make sure to evaluate how those tests go. Too often managers make mistakes and don't learn from them either because they're in denial or simply too busy to look backward.

Above all else, remain steady. Knowledge from books is a wonderful thing, but managerial competence is primarily an experiential thing – you gain it by doing rather than by being instructed. The best formula for becoming a Great Boss is a little wisdom (hopefully some of which comes from this book) and a lot of time spent in the trenches.

Is there more?

Undoubtedly there is more.

A book can shine a light on the broad strokes of a successful executive, but it can't easily reveal the subtle actions and attitudes present on a daily basis that add up to the skills of the whole person. Through some of the examples, I've tried to provide a taste of this. Unfortunately, that's as far as we can go without direct interaction. It is really up to the individual to integrate these skills into a workable package which represents them as a natural and authentic leader.

And there is little doubt that there are other, additional characteristics out there that contribute to the making of a Great Boss. As I mentioned at the outset of this book, the profiles of the extreme management styles are taken from a career's worth of careful observation of what works and doesn't work in the management field.

The profile of the Great Boss is that of a single person. Not surprisingly there are likely to be more gaps and omissions in what can and does constitute a Great Boss.

Will this guarantee me success?

Throughout the second half of this book, I've examined the various characteristics that made my Great Boss a wonderful example of managerial prowess. When you roll all these capabilities into a single individual, I hope you can see that he was both a formidable leader and a pleasure to work for.

Yet he wasn't perfect.

My Great Boss became my supervisor after he was fired from his previous job. The business he ran was sold by the corporate parent to a foreign-owned company that didn't approve of his style. Within a relatively short time, he found himself out of a job.

Which just goes to show that a boss who performs at an exceptionally high supervisory level, while having the ability to assemble and motivate a strong team and produce impressive results, can still be vulnerable if she doesn't effectively manage upward.

Being a Great Boss can be rewarding, satisfying, and even fun. But it is not enough by itself to ensure success – at least not if your goal is to climb all the way to the top of the corporate ladder.

What's next?

Most managers see themselves at some higher position on the corporate ladder sometime in their future. If that is your ambition, then the lessons contained in *Bad Boss, Great Boss* can be a great help to your progress.

They can also be a hindrance if they are substantially out of sync with your employer's culture and norms. Select carefully that which you will implement from this book if your ambition is to rise through the ranks.

Beyond becoming a great supervisor, there are two other important skills you should have in your arsenal. You will need an understanding of and the ability to utilize corporate politics to your advantage and the skills and facilities to please your boss.

Fortunately, the first topic is explored in depth in my book *Navigating Corporate Politics*. The second subject I plan to detail in an upcoming book titled *Bad Employee, Great Employee*.

How do I find my own Great Boss?

Whether you're an individual contributor looking for a new position (and consequently, a new boss) or a middle manager considering their next career move, everyone works for somebody. While I've mentioned a few strategies for identifying good bosses and avoiding extreme managers throughout the text, finding a Great Boss can be a bit tricky.

Armed with this book, you could probably devise a series of questions to ask your potential boss that would give you a pretty good picture of what it would be like.

Except it won't.

Bosses, just like most other employees, seem to be blissfully unaware of their strengths and weaknesses. And unfortunately, this ignorance can't be meaningfully translated into useful information for a job candidate to use for screening purposes. Even if the prospective manager is aware of their own style strengths and deficiencies, they aren't likely to tell you about them unless it works to their advantage. Because we know that in job interviews, everyone lies to some degree.

Still, it doesn't hurt to try.

A much better source is current subordinates of the target manager. Unfortunately, you might not know them, and they might find it too politically risky to talk to you even if they're one of your friends. In my experience, former subordinates are usually the best source of candid comments on your next potential boss. Such people are much easier to find with the advent of social media.

In addition to these sources, you can sometimes learn a lot by listening to casual comments from other interviewers – peers, other managers in the company, even recruiters on occasion. These cues are likely to be subtle but can be quite revealing if you catch the undertones present.

The bottom line is that there aren't a lot of great bosses out there. Finding a great one is a bit like searching for a needle in a haystack – you might only know you have one when it pokes you in the hand. That being said, there is still a lot of value in doing enough homework to avoid the obviously Bad Bosses.

A great opportunity reporting to a Bad Boss is no bargain.

ABOUT THE AUTHOR

Tom Spears earned a Bachelor of Science degree in Engineering from Purdue University and a Masters in Business Administration from Harvard University. He spent twenty-seven years working for four U.S.-based public corporations. During fifteen of those years, he held a title of President or Group President. Tom retired from his last Group President position in 2010 to pursue his interests in entrepreneurship and writing fiction. He is a partial owner in three small manufacturing companies and consults occasionally, having expertise in manufacturing, engineering, pricing, strategy, and corporate politics. Tom lives with his wife and four of his seven children on a rural lake in Ashland, Nebraska.

Connect with Tom Online

My website: www.tomspears.com/

Navigating Corporate Politics

Most employees find politics to be confusing, irritating, unfair, and something to be avoided at all costs. Many years in the senior management of large corporations forced me to realize ignoring politics was dangerous.

Ignoring politics makes you vulnerable. It can cost you your job. And don't even think about ascending the corporate ladder, where you'll be easily victimized by the expert politicians who lurk there.

Navigating Corporate Politics is written for those new to large corporations, those confused by the workings of their politics, or those with an emerging interest in corporate dynamics who want to learn more. It will explain how politics evolves in organizations, how to estimate the level of politics in your company, and the options you have for dealing with your employer's corporate politics.

Once you've finished, you'll be more fully equipped to understand your organization's political minefield and will have the beginnings of the skills needed to become a master politician yourself.

Other Books by Tom Spears

Fiction

<u>The Carson Series</u>
Leverage
Pursuing Other Opportunities
Outsourced (coming in 2017)

<u>The Smith Series</u>
Deliverables
Heir Apparent
Change Agent (coming in 2018)

<u>The Martin Series</u>
Incentivize
Supply Chain (coming in 2016)

<u>The Priest Series</u>
Synergy
Anergy (coming in 2018)

<u>Other/Stand Alone Novels</u>
Empowered
Right Sized (coming in 2017)